Former Pharisee

Former Pharisee: A Miraculous Journey from Legalism to Life

Copyright © 2023 Jeff Hilliard

This book is set in the typeface *Athelas* designed by Veronika Burian and Jose Scaglione.

Paperback ISBN: 9798387944758

A Publication of *Tall Pine Books*

119 E Center Street, Suite B4A | Warsaw, Indiana 46580

www.tallpinebooks.com

| 1 23 23 20 16 02 |

Published in the United States of America

FORMER PHARISEE

A MIRACULOUS JOURNEY
FROM LEGALISM
TO LIFE.

JEFF HILLIARD

Contents

To my wife, Kate. Without you this book would not exist. Your constant encouragement, wisdom, purity, and beauty have been integral in who I am today. You have sharpened and refined me. This book would be far less without your partnership. I love you.

Foreword

Jeff Hilliard has been a dear and trusted friend of mine for many years. Jeff's book "Former Pharisee" is a must read. Jeff is very vulnerable in it and lays out so much helpful information for those coming out of this perspective and those who aren't but need to understand the indoctrination one goes through to arrive at these places. It is learned and taught behavior that you begin to feel is God Himself versus a perspective. For those who grew up with this to turn away is equal to abandoning their faith. I didn't grow up in the SBC but did grow up Pentecostal and went through much of the same process but from the other side.

Jeff really hits a home run on the cost of commitment to staying with where the Holy Spirit is leading you. His life exemplifies the response to the sacrifice it takes to walk into the fullness the Holy Spirit has for us. Laying down religious culture that we believed was biblical culture is a struggle but Jeff communicates so well the kindness of the Lord to walk through that and come out in greater grace and powerful fruits of the Spirit.

Former Pharisee is not just a book about all of that alone. As you read Pastor Jeff's encounter, I know you will experience an encounter and then become an encounter. This book is an impartation of what Jeff walked out with the Lord. His response to God's glorious baptism of the Spirit by crossing the street and impacting the University campus is breathtaking! You will want to follow his lead once you digest it in these pages. This is not just a story of a SBC pastor. It's a wave of the Spirit that is being launched throughout the Body of Christ. It is the Holy Spirit crying out through these pages to every pastor, every church, everywhere, "I WANT MY CHURCH BACK!"

Buckle up and Brace for Impact!

–ROBBY DAWKINS
Equipper of the Underground Church throughout the Muslim world, Author of *Do What Jesus Did*, documentary subject and conference speaker.
www.robbydawkins.com

Preface

I WAS A SLAVE TO RELIGION. I had been a Christian for 25 years. My grandfather was a pastor and a missionary, making over 65 trips to multiple other nations. As a result of my grandfather's passion to serve God and take the Gospel message all over the world, I was given the opportunity to travel to six different countries on three continents with him. My call to serve God began to manifest at the age of 17, when my church asked me to preach a Sunday service. For the next 16 years, I progressively grew from a youth pastor into a Baptist pastor, and was very proud of who I'd become. I had preached countless sermons, led over one hundred people to Christ, and seen God move in mighty ways. Yet, in all of those accomplishments, there came a day where I realized I was merely a blind, deaf, mute who judged everyone, and was just full of hate. I need to say it was never obvious to me until one day, and it came at such a shock that I didn't really know how to respond. I found myself to be just like a Pharisee, full of judgment and rules, with Jesus suddenly in my face gently wondering, "What are you going to about it, Jeff?" The beauty, kindness, and gentleness He had with me in that moment began a journey where God began breaking the chains of religion and building a true relationship with me. The relationship He has built with me is not a master-to-servant relationship, but a friendship filled with love, patience, and deep intimacy.

Introduction

I have a degree in Christian Studies. I was taught by
theologians, wise men with eloquent speech, and I was
convinced by them to believe a certain way. I was content in
my faith. There was fruit. I strived to help people. I was
constantly focused on self-control and discipline. I was fully
committed to the religion of Christianity. I held so tightly to a
teaching point I learned in most of my classes: "Christianity has
been around for 2000 years. If you are the first person to
believe what you believe, if you are the first person to interpret
a scripture a certain way, then it's probably a good sign it is a
wrong belief or interpretation." This teaching had me believing
every revelation I ever had needed to be weighed, not only
according to the scriptures, but also according to other people. I
would read great men like Charles Spurgeon, Martin Luther, or
many other Baptists hoping to find someone who interpreted a
verse the way I had. If my search to find other people who
shared my revelation failed, then I was supposed to throw away
that new understanding.

I considered myself to be a "part-time" cessationist. Let me explain what I mean by that. A cessationist is someone who believes that Holy Spirit no longer manifests through the gifts mentioned in 1 Corinthians 12:6-11, *"There are different kinds of working, but in all of them and in everyone it is the same God at work. Now to each one the manifestation of the Spirit is given for the common good. To one there is given through the Spirit a message of wisdom, to another a message of knowledge by means of the same Spirit, to another faith by the same Spirit, to another gifts of healing by that one Spirit, to another miraculous powers, to another prophecy, to another distinguishing between spirits, to another speaking in different kinds of tongues, and to still another the interpretation of tongues. All these are the work of one and the same Spirit, and He distributes them to each one, just as He determines."* I did not believe in words of knowledge or wisdom, healing, miraculous powers, prophecy, distinguishing between spirits, tongues, or interpretation of tongues. The only gift I believed in of the nine mentioned in the passage was faith. That one is hard to deny. Without faith, it is impossible to please God, and faith comes by hearing, and hearing by the Word of God (Hebrews 11:6, Romans 10:17). This I knew, but I never saw these others, and had been taught they no longer exist. I was actually told to avoid this part of the chapter while I was pursuing my degree. I was told Holy Spirit doesn't need to do these things anymore because we have the Word of God now. As soon as Christianity is established, I was informed, Holy Spirit stops moving so much and He lets the Word lead people. I prescribed to this teaching most of my life. There were moments where this teaching was very difficult to hold on to. When I went to Third-World countries with my grandparents, I would see miracles, demons, and all kinds of manifestations of Holy Spirit. This caused me to basically concede that these places were not established Christian strongholds like the United States are. I never saw miracles here in the States. As far as the "part-time cessationist", what I mean is I knew God still moved today. I had seen way too many things happen to not believe, I just did not see them much in the U.S. Many of you may feel the same way. You don't see miracles happen. You haven't had a powerful encounter with God. Maybe, you are like the man at the beginning of this email I received recently:

Jeff, like you I was a cessationist for 42 years as a fighting fundamental Baptist pastor. I said some fairly nasty things about Charismatics...There are a lot of nutty things in the Charismatic movement... I want His balance... In case you are wondering, I saw you at a Power and Love session in Watauga, and was listening again to your testimony this AM. Thank you for your encouragement.

I also considered myself to be a 4-point Calvinist. Calvinism consists of 5 points. The acronym for Calvinism is TULIP. I never agreed with the middle point about Limited Atonement. The teaching is that Jesus only paid for the sins of the elect, but I had read Zechariah 3:9, where God declares He would remove the sins of the entire world in a single day. Many translations don't translate it this way. Most say God would remove the sin of "this land" in a single day. But the word in Hebrew is "Ha'aretz" which is the same word used in Genesis 1:1- "In the beginning, God created the Heavens and the EARTH." Therefore, in Zechariah, the declaration from God was to remove the sin of the earth in one day. I know the arguments of Calvinism. I was in agreement with the other 4 points before, but now I just see so much more than the limited view Calvinism presents about God.

BODY, SOUL AND...

The very first seed planted in me, that brought about my transformation from a Pharisee to a Follower of the Way Jesus lived, was the teachings of Watchman Nee. My grandfather loved to read his writings and he would often discuss with me his latest findings. Nee taught we are a trinity of Body, Soul, and Spirit. In college, I had been taught we are only Body and Soul, but here I was reading scripture that clearly showed we are a trinity. After a few conversations with my grandfather about it, we both accepted Nee's teaching. Inside of his trinity teaching, Nee explained how we work: the Body is a slave to sin; it is fed by the senses. The Soul is our personality and will; inside of it are our emotions and feelings. All decisions are made inside the Soul. The Spirit is connected to God; it is God's breath living inside you. Inside of it is your conscience and intuition, and through it you can commune with God.

I remember a meeting I had with my pastor at the time I was reading Watchman Nee's book "The Spiritual Man." The church had close to 200 members and he was evaluating me to see if I was suitable to help lead his youth group. He met with me for lunch to get to know me better, and to ask me doctrinal questions to feel me out for what I believed. Like me, he had been taught we are only a body and a soul. I shared with him what I had been reading, and even gave him the book. It was difficult for him to hear what I was saying, regularly interjecting about how his professors, all learned men of God, had taught him something different than what I was saying at the table. Why would he trust a 22-year-old when he probably had been taught the opposite before I was even born? When I gave him the book, he was polite and took it. I didn't expect anything, but five days later at church he stood up and preached how we are a Body, a Soul, and a Spirit. I remember being shocked at his doctrinal change. He had clearly read the book, and was publically changing his stance. This isn't a small issue, and I was well-aware a huge shift had taken place. Often times I find Christians are only presented one side of an interpretation and so they believe in it, blindly, and when the other side is presented at a later time, it is dismissed without any real consideration. This pastor had been taught one way for years, and then I brought to him something new. He listened and allowed me to give him proof, and when he examined it for himself, changed his beliefs. This is the same process that I have been doing since 2015. If the Bible proves me wrong, then who cares where I learned anything else? If we would all be like that pastor we would be much better off. I know it is difficult to take my word for anything at this point. My question is why do we take a person's word for something, and then not take someone else's, even when presented proof? Why are we so quick to believe one person, and not another?

As a result of the teachings from Watchman Nee, I did something very drastic. I learned from his book that my emotions are found inside my soul, but it is my spirit that communes with God. I knew from scripture I am supposed to worship in spirit, not soul. This brought me to the topic of music. Music is written by emotion, it is therefore soulical, not spiritual. With this information, I connected some dots. Satan could easily trap me by getting me into an emotional state and then fool me into thinking his voice was God's voice. I was so afraid of listening to the wrong voice that I took music out of my life completely for five years – the only CDs I listened to in my car were sermons. During that time I moved beyond fear and even became zealous about taking emotion out of worship not just for me, but for everyone, to the point where I pulled our church's youth worship leader aside and for 3 hours attempted to persuade him about the dangers of emotional praise music. Another time on a mission trip to the Philippines, I was brought to a church that had a praise band singing contemporary songs found on the radio. After the service I met with the leader and 2 other pastors, all at least twice my age, where I proceeded to dismantle their mode of "worship" and prove to them that only hymns were acceptable, proper worship because they have been weighed through theology. By the end of that conversation, the pastors were convinced only the hymns without musical accompaniment were acceptable by God. I was pretty determined to worship God with self-control and obedience and felt it was a personal crusade to rid the world of the falsehood of emotionally charged praise. And then I met my future wife...

Chapter 1

Strongholds

CONFLICTING CHURCHES CONFLICTING ME

She wasn't of my denomination. She didn't believe like I did. She had this passion and excitement about God, whereas I was fearful and disciplined. I always checked my excitement and never got out of control. About the time we started dating, my future wife and I alternated churches. My church was very religious (even if they didn't think so) whereas hers was not. By religious, I mean the people there were kind, but they didn't have anything to do with Holy Spirit. They never acknowledged Him, listened to Him, or let Him lead a service. I remember sitting in the balcony at my church one Sunday, when I decided to look down during the singing: everyone was standing up, still, like statues. No one swayed, no one enjoyed, and no man sang a word. The wives were holding their hymnals for their husbands to sing along with, but not a single man sang. The preaching was good, strong, and authoritative. It made me proud. Her church was in every way, the opposite. When the music started, many walked to the front of the church and openly worshipped. They sang with all their hearts. Some even danced. Everyone worshipped. And the preaching was pretty good, mostly sound in my opinion at the time, using many scriptures from all over the bible, and it was delivered with patience and kindness. Her preacher preached as if he was one of the people, not like an authority on the scriptures. I was a wreck at that church. When we walked in, I shook as few people's hands as possible, hurried to a seat, and sat down. When the music started, I would sit still, reading the Word. I didn't participate in the music. I would "talk" to God: "God can you believe all these people? They think this is what You want! They have no clue about self-control, do they? They look just like the world. It's horrible! Look at them, God. It's pathetic, the way they prance around here with no consideration for your Holiness." It was clear to me they were worshipping soulically, but they had a connection to God I envied. My only connection to God was obedience. Jesus said if you love me you'll obey (John 14:23), so I thought my obedience proved my love and devotion. They were showing me there could be more to my relationship with God, but I couldn't quite see it yet. After the worship the Pastor would preach... I would spend the whole service breaking down his points and interpretations, sometimes straining to find something wrong with his sermon so I could convince my better half to stop coming. My behavior at her church is a great example of why I called myself a Pharisee in the opening paragraph and truthfully, it got worse before it got better.

ADDRESSING THE CONFUSION

Recently, I found a message I posted on social media 2 months before my "awakening", which revealed to me just how religiously zealous I was. It shocked me, actually. The reason I initially wrote the post is I had just had a college student come into my office confused by an evangelist he saw on TV. I spent the better part of my afternoon being a good pastor, correcting and fixing the "damage" that was done. It was after that counseling session, I felt it necessary to address this growing trend I was seeing amongst our college students and young believers. Here is the post:

"The great sin of the Church today is that we have fallen victim to false teaching. We want things- some things that the Bible mentions- and we want them to be important. We skim over the parts where Scripture says they are not important. We dodge reality. We ignore God's true word, and instead believe filth that pastors preach. These things we want, they are temporary at best... health, wealth, prosperity, success, and even such as being slain in the spirit... but in the end these three remain: faith, hope (in the Lord Jesus Christ), and love. Instead of pursuing promises that someone told you... instead of holding on to (false) truths you heard a man say behind his false pulpit... hold on to those three. Build your faith! Strengthen your hope! And infinitely increase your love- for God and for your neighbor... and STOP pursuing all else."

This may or may not seem like a big deal to you but I need the intentions of my post to be clear. The very first sentence, *"The great sin of the church today is that we have fallen victim to false teaching"* is fascinating to me now because I believe it is still true, but the definition of "false teaching" has changed for me. When I wrote this in 2015, I was referring to Joel Osteen, Benny Hinn, Kenneth Copeland, and anyone else who didn't believe exactly what I was taught (by people) to believe. If they were not Baptist, they were false. (I still don't believe all that these men say and teach currently, but I also haven't found anyone else who believes everything I do). They are still teaching Jesus is the only way to heaven, they honor God to best of their ability. It doesn't matter if their mode of honoring God is the same as mine, their heart is the same. Paul wrote, in 3 different letters, even if someone preaches a different Jesus than what I preach, as long as Christ is proclaimed (2 Corinthians 11:4, 1 Corinthians 1:23, Philippians 1:18), I rejoice. I still think the problem the Church has today is false teaching, but I don't think the problem are these men, or any person. False teaching is when we say Jesus didn't die on the cross and rose again; if he didn't die on that cross and resurrect, now we have a false teacher (Philippians 1:18). I have heard so many Sunday school teachers, pastors, and godly men and women, when asked about a teaching that contradicts a scripture, answer with a commonly themed response: "Oh that takes a certain level of spiritual maturity to understand. I know what you think you read in that verse, but it doesn't mean what it says." Why? Why does it mean something different than it says? What if it means exactly what it says? Could it be that God actually said what He meant? I now believe this saying is dangerous because I've learned people used it in my past to manipulate people. Clearly, some passages of scripture are coded and meant to be taken figuratively. Other passages of scripture are meant to be interpreted spiritually. But for the most part, scripture doesn't have to be interpreted. It means what it says. We must realize the enemy is the one who twists scripture to get us to believe lies. God is not the one who manipulates. I hope we all consider this and become cautious, careful that we aren't causing people to stumble. I have come to realize *our enemy is not flesh and blood, but instead we fight against principalities, against powers, against the rulers of the darkness of this world, against spiritual forces of wickedness in high places* (Ephesians 6:12). The problem is Spiritual. We have an enemy, and he knows the Word. He can quote it to us, and if we don't know it well, we miss how he changes it and corrupts it to trick us. I have always believed that, but in my past I would struggle in my execution of remembering that people are not the problem.

MAKE NO MAN YOUR TEACHER

Satan knows the scriptures and he has manipulated our understanding in a way that too many Christians read their bible with teachings that are short of the truth and intention of God. Jesus taught no man should teach. He said we should not call any man our teacher, yet we often ask each other for help with a scripture we struggle to understand. I was taught by professors I should always read commentaries and books to help me understand; spending a minimum of 10 hours researching and reading about a scripture before I preached. I did this for years, typically spending close to 30 hours a week studying scripture, reading other sermons and commentaries in order to have a doctrinally sound sermon on Sunday. Since my transformation and "awakening," I no longer go to men for answers or help. I only go to God. I am learning how to hear God clearly, and I depend on Him to help me understand a scripture when I lack enough wisdom. Also, I no longer study scriptures to preach. I constantly study scriptures to apply what I read to my life. Now, I only read with that purpose, and I read constantly. "God, show me how to apply this. Show me your character so I can become a more accurate Ambassador," is often my prayer. And I now spend approximately 40 hours a week in the Word, constantly trying to see new things and look at a scripture from a new angle, asking God for more and more revelation.

Instead of reading Spurgeon or Luther, I now read scripture. I don't ask other pastors, I ask God. I am continually overwhelmed by His clarity and His urgency to answer my questions. I believe this is a major issue with the Church today.

Pastors are not going to God, but are going to men for understanding instead. Jesus said you will know a false teacher by
their fruit. *A good tree cannot bear bad fruit, and bad tree
cannot bear good fruit* (Matthew 7:18). I used to think people
like Benny Hinn were false teachers. I told people he was a
false prophet because I didn't understand anything I saw
happen in his ministry. Watching 500 people fall down (a.k.a.
"slain in the spirit") in a crowd of 7,000 just seemed manufac-
tured and staged to me. I thought people coming up on the
platform with testimonies of healing were paid actors. I was
focused on the one man I saw in a wheelchair not get out of it
and not be healed in that moment because I was caught up in
the teachings I was raised in which said "if someone really is a
healer, everyone would get healed and there would be no failure, not one". It was the same for healing, prophecy, anything.
If someone was claiming to have a ministry for God it had to
done to perfection; if God is perfect and He is using someone,
then He should use them perfectly. That was my thought, and
maybe you've been taught that or believed it yourself. I used to
think the Matthew 7:15-23 passage of the good or bad tree was
Jesus referring to people who do miracles as their main focus of
ministry as false teachers. I no longer believe that because God
has showed me more scripture and taught me how Jesus clari-
fied His Matthew 7 teaching in Matthew 12:25-37. He teaches
us that good "fruit" is bringing out the good things God has
stored up inside the man. Jesus wasn't talking about sin. Jesus
wasn't talking about miracles or ministry. Jesus was talking
about producing evidence of God's love and Kingdom from the
blessings and promises that have been stored up inside a man's
spirit. God is very active today, and I believe He is waiting for
us to get aligned with His will so He can bless us. So often we
go to men for advice for clarification, and they give us their
opinion, like David in 1 Chronicles 13 who asked the priests

and the people "if it sits well with you we will move the ark in the city", and it seemed like wisdom but it wasn't, and God's anger burned at them and a man (Uzzah) dies because they never sought the Lord to ask if they should bring His Presence, in the Ark, to the city. Make no man your teacher is what I continually teach my congregation at our church. If they have a question I tell them to go to Him. My job as a pastor is not to answer people's questions, but to teach them how to have a conversation with God so they can ask Him their questions.

FALSE TEACHERS TO FRIENDS

The next part of my post on social media was *"We want things...and we want them to be important."* I was intentionally being vague in my post, but I was referring to a whole bunch of topics. For example, when I wrote, "things" I meant healing, deliverance, money, and freedom. Who doesn't want to be healed? Who doesn't want to be delivered from demons? Who doesn't want to be stress free? Who doesn't want more money? We all do, but that doesn't mean God is going to give them to you. Sin creates punishment. You are sick, you have demons, you have stress, mental illness, or you have financial problems because of your sin. This was my stance when I wrote this in 2015, and it still is. But it is also different now. You see, I was conveniently leaving out God's will in 2015. I was forgetting about Satan and God. I thought our choices had repercussions. I was avoiding 1 Corinthians 13:5, where it says *"love keeps no records of wrongs,"* or 2 Corinthians 5:19, where it says *"that God was reconciling the world to himself in Christ, not counting men's sins against them."* (NIV) If God doesn't count our sins against us, if He keeps no records of our wrongs, then repercussions are not valid. I was forgetting about Justification. Romans 8:30, for example says, *"And those he predestined, he also called; those he called, he also justified...*" The word justification is spectacular. Justification means to be reset, as if I never sinned. If I have been justified, then my sins have been erased, and is that not the Gospel? It's why we call it Good News. We can't forget that. I had forgotten it. I had listened to too many people tell me what they thought was right; I thought that freedom from sin, sickness, depression, demons, and whatever else you can think of was far less important to God compared to doctrine. I thought God wanted me to teach about religious theories and religious discipline. I missed the part where Jesus came to set people free from sin, sickness, depression, demons, and whatever else you want to add to the list. I ignored that the bible says people lined up for hours to receive freedom when Jesus was in town. I missed that Jesus rarely entered a town, because people would meet Him outside the city. I had forgotten that at one time, He taught and ministered for three days without eating.

I didn't understand how the Pharisees were consumed with religious theories and doctrines, and how they hated Jesus because He could care less about what they did. After all, He told everyone to do what the Pharisees said, but not to do what they did. I was wrong about so many things. Jesus made freedom important. I missed Isaiah 61, where it says he had a message to preach, proclaiming freedom for the captives. Jesus didn't miss it. He quoted it in Luke 4, saying He was the fulfillment of that passage. Yes, sin exists, demons exist, and there are bad things in life... but God is not the source of those things. Jesus was clear about that when he said John 10:10. *"The thief comes to steal, kill, and destroy..."* What I meant in my post was the prosperity teachings are false doctrine and the preachers who make that their message were false teachers. I was addressing our desires to prosper, and I was suggesting that God gives and He takes away because Job said so, despite the fact that Jesus said otherwise. I didn't realize that the verse after Job's famous quote says God didn't count it as sin when Job said it. Although I am still not convinced about the prosperity gospel, I no longer consider these preachers to be false teachers. It would be wrong to do so, because that would be an incorrect interpretation of the Matthew 12 passage. The "hyper-grace" prosperity gospel group and I disagree on a lot of things. However, my desire is to avoid labeling someone a false teacher if I have never sat down with them and heard them share their heart and reasons behind what they say. I want to be slow to judge people. I want to be quick to listen. Anyone can make a video cut up of someone else talking and "expose" them for mistakes. It is done all the time. However, it is important that we ask questions and get to know someone, because it is in conversations with people that they become human, and someone you would label a "false teacher" might actually become a friend.

THESE THINGS ARE TEMPORARY

"These things are temporary at best." Under my old way of thinking, this was very true. Life is fleeting, things change, and nothing lasts forever – except God, His promises, and us. Let me tell you more about me: I was clinically diagnosed as manic bipolar in 2006, I've battled demons in my past (I have a similar past as Kris Vallotton), and I was severely injured in the Fall of 2000. So I had constant stress, and I was in constant pain. I didn't believe in healing, so how could I ever hope for a permanent fix and rest from my daily struggles? Life was pretty hard for me. Each day was torture. For 14+ years, I would wake up in physical pain, look myself in the mirror and loath who I saw, and wish God would just "take me home." That's why I wrote that health, wealth, prosperity, and success were temporary at

best. I didn't know I could hope enough to pursue what I needed from God. I settled for allowing a headache to linger, taking a pill to relieve physical pain. Believing the pain was God's will for me, or He was trying to teach me a lesson so I could manage the temporary pain because it is wrong to question God. Even if I had pain now in my mortal body, all pain would die when I die; it was this mentality that helped me cope, as exhausting and hopeless as it was, and led me to write such a sad and hopeless statement. Looking back, I don't know how I never saw the flaws of my wrong beliefs. What fruit was I producing? Where was joy? Where was hope? Hope is a must in the Kingdom of God. How did I think hopelessness was okay?

WHEN HOLY SPIRIT TOUCHES

"...even such as being slain in the spirit..." I wanted to believe in the Presence of God. I knew Moses had experienced it. I knew about Daniel and his three friends. I knew about Acts 2. I knew about Saul/Paul. I even knew one time Christ revealed Himself to me in a way that I felt His presence so strongly that I stood up in a room with 350 other kids about my age, even though I didn't want to stand up. I was 15 years old, it was my birthday, and I was at a Christian Summer Camp. I hadn't felt God in so long, I hadn't heard His voice in so long, and I was really lonely. The preacher was evangelizing with all he had in him, and I was sitting there listening. He gave an invitation. I had been a Christian for about 8 years, but I wasn't living any different than the rest of the world. I began to try to talk to Jesus in my head, and then I said a simple statement, "If you are real, I need to feel you right now." Immediately, I felt the hair on my head and neck stand up, as if I had static electricity, and then my body just stood up. The preacher was still talking, so when I

stood up he wasn't ready for me. He stumbled on his words and everyone laughed and looked at me. I was terrified, but I couldn't move. It was a very holy moment, and it gave me critical evidence for His presence, that He truly does things like this in which we cannot rationalize or logically dismiss. I wish I had pursued His tangible presence fully from that moment on, instead of waiting 18 years. I knew being slain in the spirit was biblical and possible. For example, when those from the Sanhedrin came to arrest Jesus in the garden, and they ask if he was the man and Jesus replied, "I am he" the soldiers, chief priests and Pharisees drew back and fell to the ground. The problem was I had seen so many people I assumed were faking being slain. I thought it was a learned behavior people do to manipulate others. I still think sometimes people fake it. I don't know why they do that. When I lay hands on people now, I feel when Holy Spirit touches them and when He doesn't. I may lay hands on 50 people, but feel 15 get touched, and other times all 50 get touched. Seeing people do down because it is expected, or worse seeing the evangelist or pastor try to physically use force to bring people to the floor was and still is a big issue for me. I truly don't like it. Even more, it gives people, like who I was when I wrote this post, the excuse to ridicule people and actually miss a true opportunity to be touched by the power of God themselves. Every time we give someone the excuse to dismiss the power of God, we are damaging the body of Christ. I will get into my transformation later, but you will see that at the moment of my transformation I was alone with God. Every time I have growth in the Spirit, I am alone with God, and definitely not because someone laid hands on me. I have been slain multiple times since the most pivotal moment of my walk with God, in my secret place and in churches, both without someone touching me and with human interaction. I think there is a culture in some churches that encourages people to be slain in the spirit. It's as if there is a pressure to go down, an expectation that when a certain person touches you, you are supposed to fall. That is not healthy. People so desperately want a touch of God to move powerfully in their lives, and they will do whatever it takes. Sometimes, they will even fake it in hopes to somehow move God to act. But let's be clear, if when you fall down, you get up the same person without any transformation, then something is wrong. When God touches you, you will never be the same again. I do not allow myself to go down, ever. The only way I go down is because God hits me so intensely that I cannot stand up.

I want to encourage you to pursue more of God. Never settle for the status quo. Push yourself to the point of failure, and risk looking like a fool. Be desperate! In Acts 22:11, Paul explained the glory of God had blinded him on the road to Damascus, and that the glory had transformed him. He was a changed man from that moment. Paul used the word "doxa" for glory. And when I search scriptures, I have found that when Doxa Glory hits a person, they are changed. I think too often we settle for the simple prayer and anointing that someone carries instead of tarrying for the presence of God. His presence is far greater than any anointing I have ever come in contact with. But too often, we feel the presence of God in that anointing and so we fall without having a real encounter with the Doxa glory presence of God that transforms us.

A few years ago, we had a woman from another church start attending one of our small groups. She and her husband were loyal and traditional Baptists. She was truly enjoying her time with the group, learning some new things, being in awe of some of the things God was doing in the group. He, on the other hand, was not happy about it. So, one night he decided to come up to the church during the small group meeting. I had not met him, and honestly had no clue any of this was going on.

At the end of the lesson, the group of about 20 people split up into smaller groups and began to pray for each other. I noticed a few of the guys went outside, but never thought anything of it. Suddenly, one of the men that went outside came running back inside and told me, "Jeff! (The woman's husband) is outside and he is here to fight you! He is really angry and determined to put a stop to everything right now!" I was shocked, but at the same time, I knew he had never met me. I felt the Lord nudge me to go outside, so I did. I found the husband yelling at one of our other guys who was trying to calm him down. I just walked up and joined the conversation. I didn't introduce myself or anything like that, just started talking. We calmed him down a little, actually had him laughing about random things, and just got him to relax. He was still determined to beat up the pastor, but he thought we were cool guys. As soon as he said as much, I reached out my hand and said, "Hey, it's really nice to meet you, I didn't catch your name yet, and I haven't introduced myself. My name is Pastor Jeff. I'm the guy you came to beat up tonight." The whole thing caught him off guard. We had been talking for quite some time, and suddenly he realized who I was. He retreated, "No, no, no, I would never..." I interrupted, "It's okay, sometimes we do things without thinking. More than that, you've never met me until now, so I never expected you to like me or be okay with something so new or different. But you've been hearing my heart on a lot of things, and I just want you to listen to my perspective..." I went on to explain some more things to him, and it was a great conversation. Then we began to talk about getting slain in the spirit and all the abuses we've seen and heard about. We both agreed on that, but then I began to tell him about some of the more beautiful experiences I've had. He was intrigued. I asked him if I could pray for Holy Spirit to touch him. He agreed, so I put my hand on his chest and said, "Holy Spirit, he loves you, but is afraid of what you can do. Show him your beauty through your power." He closed his eyes and fell backwards. By then there were 3 guys outside who helped catch him so he wouldn't hit his head on the parking lot pavement. As soon as he went down, I continued the prayer, "Holy Spirit, don't let him get up the same man that fell down." His wife came running outside, yelling, "What did you do? What happened?" and I smiled and said, "I just introduced him to Holy Spirit." She got excited and asked if I would pray for her, too, so I did, and she went down beside them. I still have the picture of them laying in our parking lot as a reminder of what God can do.

JOINING THE PHARISEE RANKS

"...*false pulpit*..." Those are pretty strong words. As you can see, I didn't have a lot of love in my heart for false prophets hiding behind their false pulpits. I considered them my enemy. I spent so much time teaching against them, correcting what they were "messing up". Of course, I never listened to them. I wanted nothing to do with them. The Pharisees called Jesus a false prophet, and it led them to kill Him. It was when I read this part of my old post that I began to cry. I know I was a Pharisee. I would have put Jesus on the cross. I would have stoned Stephen. I would have joined Saul in hunting them down. I wanted to remove people like Benny Hinn from ministry. I believed he (and his entire family) was going to hell. I hated these men, and women. How sad...how very little love I had in my heart... I haven't met a person, yet, who was more zealous than I was in March 2015. I was passionately aggressive, for the god I knew (yes, the little "g" is on purpose). I now know that I didn't know God. I knew OF Him, but not personally. In that way, I was a lot like Job (read the beginning of chapter 42 of Job). I heard His voice from time to time, and every once in a while, I would encounter Him on a small level. But the god I really knew was Religion. My god hated false prophets, He was going to send them all to hell and watch them burn for their treachery and damage they did to His Kingdom.

In October, 2011, I went to Thailand, Laos, and the Philippines. In Thailand, I was invited (along with the other 2 men I was ministering with) to attend a conference. We were being hunted in Laos for preaching the Gospel and had to be escorted across the border to escape the communists. So we went to this conference for a few days until the heat died down. The conference started amazingly, with a powerful procession and worship. And then, Holy Spirit came into the huge room where about 800 Thai and Lao people were worshipping. Suddenly, many began to dance and roll on the floor, most erupting into tongues. I didn't recognize Holy Spirit, and instead assumed this was demonic. I looked at the other missionaries and the leader of the group for advice, and I could feel my zeal rising within me. I was ready to grab a microphone and put an end to this nonsense, but our leader calmed me down and told me to go outside and pray. When I walked outside, immediately my zeal stopped and the god I knew left me. I now know it wasn't God, at all. It was Religion, a wicked Spirit indeed, and I misidentified Holy Spirit as a demonic spirit when He actually entered the room. I always thought the main gift of the Fruit of the Spirit was *physical* self-control, and in my mind that meant no emotion when worshipping, no acting foolish, but being stoic, reverent. I don't know why I could not understand self-control was spiritual, when it's a Fruit of the Spirit it has to be spiritual. The Pharisees called Jesus a false prophet, just like I called Holy Spirit false when I encountered His presence because I misunderstood the scriptures and made the same mistakes they did. I couldn't even recognize Holy Spirit, the one part of the whole Trinity I am supposed to work with, came into the room. I completely missed it. I used to think the Pharisees were crazy, because they knew the Father but didn't know Jesus. It was evident that even though I knew Jesus I didn't know Holy Spirit – I didn't know the 3 Persons of God. That's why I was missing wholeness.

If you are reading this and thinking "how could you misidentify Holy Spirit so much you thought it's from the devil?" I don't have an answer for you. All I can tell you is, Jeff on February 11, 2015 would hate me now. He would do all he could to stop me from writing this book. People often say things like "if my 6-year-old-self saw me today, he would hate me." Well, Jeff from before April 2015 would want me dead, just like the Pharisees wanted Jesus dead. Even though that Jeff would hate me, I love that Jeff. He didn't know what he didn't know. He was so close to discovering the truth. Jesus was about to do a miracle in his life.

I CAN FIX IT

After I got back from my run-in with Holy Spirit in Asia, my (now) wife and I continued for another 3 years, shuffling between her Pentecostal church and whichever church I was preaching at (I filled in for multiple churches for almost 3 full years). Slowly, I convinced her that certain parts of her church's teachings were wrong. I fixed her. I was proud of my service to God, to fix what Satan had been working so hard to do in her life. Slowly, her excitement and enthusiasm for God dwindled to a slow crawl. In that time, she became my wife. My influence had really taken hold of her. I became a pastor of a small church; and by small I mean 12 members in the entire congregation. I worked hard to identify any problems the church might have had, and obviously there were a few on the list with such a dwindling crowd. I was diligent in my work to remove all emotion and unbiblical excitement. I was fully content; feeling I was fulfilling what God had called me to do to create this atmosphere of religion and clear doctrine. I taught about how we are to love others. We talked a lot about love. And we talked some more about it....and we talked. There was very little practice involved. We grew a little and it was great, we all worked hard together to grow. They were amazing people to pastor. About 10 months into my time at the church, on March 15, 2015, a college student sent me a video of a man teaching on what I had come to know was ridiculous and utter nonsense. To be more specific, he was teaching about healing and that a prayer of faith is heard and answered by God. I had been taught that a prayer is only part of the deciding factor God uses in order to make a decision. I believed, as many others still do that God *can* do anything, but He doesn't always *want* to. I would hear and say the common phrase "I know you can God, but will you?" This man on a YouTube video was teaching that "Yes! God wants to heal! Faith is all that He needs."

OUT OF MY CONTROL

The college student who forwarded me the 19 minute video sent a question along with it: "What do you think of this guy?" My answer was telling... "He's cooler than I will ever be." I thought his sermon was nonsense, stupid and pointless, but he looked cool and I was sure he would have lots of people follow his false teaching because it sounded nice. I watched the sermon again because there was something in me that had to hear it again. Then the next day, I watched it again. This continued for a few days, until my wife came home from work, on March 21, with a DVD. She said, "A friend was telling me about this video the other day and I think we will enjoy it." I watched it, and for the next week, I was so confused. The DVD was a documentary filming miracles of God across the world titled "Holy Ghost." I could not understand how anyone could document these events and say they were of God. It was amazing. They were doing impossible things and they did them in the name of Jesus, only. Everything was through Jesus. I was blown away by the whole thing, it didn't make sense. What made it worse was that guy from the shared video who was cooler than I will ever be was actually in the documentary!!! I was FILLED with anger and confusion. I threw the remote across the room, and I demanded my wife turn the filth off. My understanding of God was damaged, "God, why would you allow such a documentary to be made? It goes against everything you are and want. Surely this is wrong. And how could you allow THAT guy to be in it???" And then the next day, "God, that video goes against everything I have come to know to be true! Why did you allow this?" By the end of a week's time, I was talking to my wife, "I don't understand. This is tearing me up inside. Everything I know was destroyed in that video. Every rule, every understanding, everything I know— gone. God doesn't respond to my prayers like He did to their prayers."

Chapter 2

Awakened

RESURRECTION SUNDAY

Weeks went by. I could find no rest. Easter, 2015, was approaching. On March 8, 2015, I had made a statement in one of my sermons, "Easter is four weeks away. Wouldn't it be great if, in four weeks, our church celebrated it's resurrection on the same day we celebrate Jesus'?" Everyone clapped and said amen because of the fragile state of our church. In the 80s, our church was the fastest growing church in South Texas, they averaged 135 people every week, baptisms were constant, the church was full of life. The people who had been loyal and never gave up on the church watched it slowly die for thirty years and were powerless to stop it. The idea of a revitalized church sounded amazing, but we had no clue what it meant. So Easter morning came, April 5, 2015. We had a Sunrise Service and it was great.... except for one thing: nothing happened. There was no change. We stayed the same. I went home, rested, and forced myself to stop thinking about it. On Tuesday, April 7, I went to the church. I was sitting at my desk, thinking about everything. There in my office chair God said to me, "Jeff, you said you were going to change. You said you were going to celebrate newness. I held up my end, but you didn't." I was shocked. I hadn't heard a voice like that very often in my life. I had no answer for it. Suddenly, I thought of that stupid video the student had sent me almost a month earlier. I watched it again; the man was so sure of what he was teaching. Then I thought of the documentary. I did some research on it, and found it was only one part of a series of documentaries. I bought the whole series. I went on the internet and looked up more on this guy, Todd White, the man from the original video and the documentary which had turned my world upside down. He had hundreds of videos. He was out in the streets, he was in churches. It didn't matter, he was everywhere. More importantly, he was so sure about what he taught. I was convicted. I saw a man who had no training, no background, but he was going out into the streets telling anyone and everyone, "Jesus loves you." He prayed for a kid with a broken wrist, and when he finished the prayer he said, "Check it out dude." The kid moved his hand inside his cast and then cussed out loud. He cussed! So this guy, Todd, prayed and said "Thank you Jesus that you love us. Wrist, I command you be healed in Jesus name." And the kid got healed right there, and then he cussed! Doesn't that mean God knew he was going to cuss once He healed him? Yes it does. My brain went bananas, "So did God heal him anyway?" Yes He did. "So does that mean God wanted a relationship with the kid so much that He looked past the reaction?" Yes, without a shadow of a doubt. I was more than convicted. I went outside my office. God told me to go.

"IF IT WILL HELP"

I opened the door to step outside and fear grabbed hold of me...
I looked around (extremely fearful and nervous to share the
gospel on the street, outside my church), saw no one, and told
God, "Well, I came out here. You should've sent someone to
me. You didn't, so I'm going back inside to work." God wouldn't
let me back inside. I looked around and saw our empty trashcans out on the street. "Okay, God. I'm going to go walk to
those trashcans. If I see someone out here, I will talk to them,
but if you don't send them, it's on you." So I began to walk. By
my third step, I saw a young man walking toward me. I scram-
bled in fear, "God, if he doesn't get to the trashcan by the time I
do, it's on you." I sped up my pace to a brisk walk, but something amazing happened. He did to! So I slowed down, and so
did he! I had only one choice left, I gave up and walked
normal...we arrived at the trashcans at the exact same moment.
I took a deep breath to say something like, "How are you
doing?" and instead all I did was freak out inside. You see, he
was very obviously a Muslim, full beard, dressed in a long black
robe with gold patterns and a black, Muslim hat on his head. I
held my breath, looking directly into his eyes, and nodded my
head, turned around, and started dragging the cans back to
where they go. But as I turned away from him, I heard him say
something.

"I have a test."

"Excuse me?" I asked.

He pointed to the university across the street and repeated
his earlier statement, "I have a test."

"Oh!" I said, "You are about to take a test."

"Yes," he replied.

I left the trashcans in the middle of the parking lot and
began to walk with him towards the school. His name was

Ahmed, he was a graduate student, and he was about to take an extremely important test. He informed me that he had to make an A on the test in order to make a grade high enough to continue his education. If he made a B on the test, his overall grade would result in a C and he would be kicked out of school, sent back to Pakistan.

"Can I pray for you?" I asked.

"Why would you pray?" he wondered out loud.

I answered, "Because I believe my God loves you and wants a relationship with you. I believe He will help you."

"But I am Muslim. Why would you pray?"

"Because I love you and want you to know my God."

We continued walking; he explained further that there was no hope for him. He could not pass this test at all. He had already packed his luggage in anticipation of the impending result.

I answered, "Well, I believe God will help you. He is a loving Father."

His reply was shocking to me, "Yes, you can pray."

"Now Ahmed, you must know I am going to pray to Jesus. He is my God. I am going to ask Jesus to help you."

He looked down, then back up at me in an instant, shrugged and said, "If it will help."

So I prayed. My prayer was new to me, "Jesus, help Ahmed make a 100 on his test today so that he knows you love him and that you are God. In Jesus' name, amen." I had never prayed with such certainty. He said amen, shook my hand and walked away. I sat down on the front steps of the church. I prayed for over 100 people that afternoon. I cried all the way home that evening.

IF THAT HEATHEN CAN DO IT

The next day, I was excited to get to the church to watch more videos of the same man doing street ministry. Video after video, person after person, of this one man loving people, praying for people, and seeing God answer the prayers. Then came the video that changed me...he was in a city known for sin. As he was walking, a man approached.

Todd spoke up, "You have back problems, sir. My God can heal you."

"Uh, yeah, man. How did you know? Are you psychic?"

"No I am not, but God lives in me, and He knows you. He told me about your back. Let me pray." Todd replied.

So he had the guy sit down. You see, the guy's right leg was shorter than his left by about 4 inches. So he grabbed the guy's ankles and prayed, "Thank you Jesus..." Before he could say anything else, the leg began to grow. He still finished the prayer, but like I said, the leg was already growing. I tried to rationalize the whole thing by saying it was camera tricks. I watched it again, slowing down the speed of the footage so I could better study it. The camera never moved, and even worse the guy never moved. Nothing moved, except the leg that was shorter now wasn't. I was stunned, and even more I had to test this out for myself.

The reason I wanted to test it out was because I was paralyzed in a high school football game. There were a lot of reasons why I was paralyzed, but there are 2 important reasons to note: one, my right leg has always been 1 inch shorter than my left leg. I first noticed the problem when I was around 5 years old. I remember watching TV at my grandparents' house and I pulled my knees to my chest and tried to rest my chin on them. When I did, I realized my chin rested crookedly. From then on, I was always aware of the length issue. I eventually went to a chiropractor and he confirmed the whole thing and gave me an insert for me to put in my right shoe. Two, I tackled a guy really hard in a football game five weeks before the paralysis, and tore the muscle in my lower back. The torn muscle caused a problem and basically my legs quit working for a few minutes. Add another 15 years to the issue and I had become a guy with two 90 degree angles in my spine, and with the left side of my abs no longer working. I could no longer use my abs to do sit ups or even to go to the bathroom. It took me between 20 and 30 minutes to urinate, and much longer to do the rest because I couldn't push. To say the least, I had a few problems on the morning of April 8th, 2015, and I was sitting there at my desk watching a man, with bigger problems than me, getting prayer from a guy who believes in stuff I just knew to be wrong; and he was healed!! So right there in my judgmental state I pushed my chair back, looked at my legs, and said to God, "If that heathen can do it, then so can I." So then I said out loud, "Right leg, I command you to grow in Jesus' name." I felt an immediate tingle in my right shin, just below my knee. It was weird. Then, in the next second, I felt my heel digging into the floor. I looked at my ankle and saw my leg growing out of my pants! That was it. It finished there. I looked down; my legs were the exact same length. And then I heard God speak...

"Stand up and check your back."

So I stood up, scared. Then He said to me, "Touch your toes."

I replied, "God, you know I can't touch my toes. I haven't been able to do that in 15 years."

He told me again. I denied His command. He stated it a third time. I bent down and my palms hit the floor! If the floor hadn't been there, honestly, I could have gone farther. I stood up, in tears. God wasn't done though. He continued and said "Now turn left..." You see, I hadn't been able to turn left since September 2000. My muscles that should have turned my torso left were dead. The nerves, or whatever it is that gives the directions, were severed and dead. My spine was so twisted and curved it could not twist left without severe pain, and even that required help to do. I used to go to chiropractors twice a week at 5:00 am to have them try to straighten my back and slow down the deterioration of my spine. It was brutal agony. So when God told me to "Turn left" I was against even the thought of it. I tried to explain to God that it was impossible for me to do so. He repeated His command... I, again, explained my position. Then, God said in an audible voice, "Jeff, I am not asking you. Turn left now!" Yes, it was audible, which is terrifying by the way. I knew what I had to do. I braced myself for pain, wound up as far to the right as I could in order to pull myself left, and then let go. My back popped 8 times. I felt the pops as they started at the base of my spine and popped up until the last, behind my lungs. I turned left, easily, without resistance, for the first time in a decade. I cried. Fifteen years of pain with over 10 years of increasingly limited mobility were no longer relevant because He had healed me. I worshipped God with all I had. He is amazing. He healed me, my leg, and my back. I kept looking down and checking. I noticed little things, such as my belly button. Over 15 years, it had slowly moved to the right and sat about 2 inches over on my right side for the last few years, but on the morning of April 8, 2015, it was straight. Then, I heard God say, "Freely I have given you, now freely give." I went out on the street corner and prayed for everyone I could. That night, at our church's prayer meeting, I told everyone about my back. My mom was there. Before I started speaking, she asked me what was different. When I told them the story she shouted, "I got it! You're taller!" On April 7, 2015, I was 5'10.5". As of April 8, I am 6'0". Between my leg growing out and my spine straightening, I grew an inch and a half.

"YES, I KNOW"

Thursday morning, April 9th, I arrived early to the church. I finished all my work by 9:00 a.m., sent out a text to some of the college students who attended our church, and invited them to join me in praying for everyone we could who passed by the church. We set up shop on the street corner, with ice chests full of bottled water. I had begun a fast on Wednesday so all I was ingesting was water and the Word. There were three students who joined me out there, and the four of us prayed for over 400 students that day. It was amazing as God was healing people, blessing them, helping them, and showing Himself to them. Over 150 gave their life to Jesus throughout the day. Then, I saw Ahmed. I hadn't seen him since Tuesday when I had prayed. He was trying to hide himself, wearing American clothes and a hat, with shades on, carrying his backpack over his right shoulder.

I shouted out in joy, "Ahmed! Did you receive your grade for that test, yet?"

He looked up, through his sunglasses. I could see fear all over his face. He nodded, while trembling slightly. Everyone stopped. There were about 15 people there at the time. All eyes were on him. I asked, "And how did you do?"

It seemed like ages past as he struggled to pull in a breath... He slowly brought his right hand up to his shades, only to delicately pull them down, just below his eyes. He froze, completely still for a moment, and as fast as he could make himself say it, he exclaimed,

"I made a hundred!" Ahmed fled in fright. He ran out into the street to escape any more questions.

I shouted his name, "Ahmed! Ahmed! You know it was because of Jesus, right?"

He stopped, turned around towards us and the crowd. There were tears running down his face. He was broken. He forced himself together as he said in the quietest voice he could, "Yes, I know." And with that, he walked home. I have never seen Ahmed since that day, but the story doesn't end there.

I had invited a student who went to our church to come pray with us that day that wasn't one of the other three I previously mentioned. He was like I had been, he didn't believe God answered prayers simply because we asked. He believed God can, but doesn't always want to. I had changed and I knew that was untrue. I had seen God say yes to prayers, regardless of the faith or necessity, because God had healed me despite the fact that I was trying to prove Todd wrong when I commanded my leg to grow out. But this young man, stood out there for hours with us. He never prayed for a single person, but simply shook his head "no" every time I invited him to join us. He was there when Ahmed walked by.

"THIS IS NOT LOVE"

At 4:00 p.m., our group was tired, exhausted, and out of bottles of water, so we went to my office to discuss what we had seen. The students who had been praying were ecstatic. They had dreamed of days like this, where God said yes to our petitions and revealed Himself to the masses. The other student, well, he scolded us and informed us of our fallacy. After the discussion, I drove home. At midnight, I received a phone call from the "skeptic". He had been at a bible study on campus after our time together, and called me to tell me what happened.

I woke up and answered, "Hello?"

There was silence for a moment before I heard, "I am sorry."

"Sorry about what?" I asked.

"I was wrong."

"What were you wrong about? I am confused."

He said, "About earlier. I said what y'all were doing was not what God wants. I told you that you were forcing Jesus on them, that it wasn't love. I was wrong."

"Okay, so you were wrong. Why do you say that?"

"Because you need to know what happened at the bible study tonight, Jeff."

"Well, what happened?"

"We were having bible study, and were almost done. Then all of a sudden, there was a loud banging on the door. Five men came into the room, a Muslim and four Hindus. They came in very brashly. The Muslim man said, 'We have questions!' The leader of the Bible study stood up and said, 'I think I have the answers.' Jeff, that's when I recognized the Muslim as the man that scored the 100 on the test. He said, 'Okay, there is a crazy white man standing on the corner down the street. He is praying for everyone about anything. But everything he prays happens. Why? Who is Jesus?'"

I was shocked...I never would have imagined that. There was silence on the phone, until he said one last thing to me, "Jeff, we told them about Jesus. They all accepted Christ tonight and renounced their old ways. I was wrong."

LOVE TRULY CASTS OUT FEAR

I was speechless. I hadn't anticipated anything like that. I simply wanted to show people God loved them. What I found most amazing through this whole experience was God was different than what I had thought. I had always thought God needed us to fear Him and to repent out of fear. I don't know if I had been purposefully taught to think this way, but when I look back at all the teaching in Sunday School and Vacation Bible School, summer camps, bible studies, youth events, college...I see that everything was surrounded by fear. Even my respect of God was rooted in fear. I was taught to repent from my sin because if I didn't, I would be punished (maybe unable to speak to God, separated, bound for hell).

I was taught that if I didn't pray for God to forgive my sins each day, that God couldn't hear any of my prayers because the sins would prevent it. I mean, I was even encouraged by church leaders to accept Jesus so I didn't go to hell: "How many of you want to go to hell? Well, if you don't, you need to say this prayer and repeat after me." Who wouldn't want to say that prayer? No one wants to go to hell. But the motivation to pray this way is fear. The Word of God says that it is His goodness that leads men to repentance, not fear (Romans 2:4). His love should be the motivation for everything in my life, especially my relationship with Him.

So back to what I learned from the phone call and encounter...I saw God was in love with me, with everyone. He was not concerned about the difficulty in breaking through these five non-Christians' backgrounds, their nationalities, their religions. He loved them and wanted them to love Him, so He was answering our prayers and showing these people He was real, that Jesus was real. We were not out there with picket lines and posters protesting, yelling, condemning people, saying, "Repent or go to hell!" We were out on the corner, sitting in the shade with an ice chest full of water, saying, "Would you like some water? Is there anything I can pray for, to ask God to help you with? Is there anything at all?" That was it. We prayed in Jesus' name. We were clear as to whom we were praying, and I was amazed. God was so gentle. He answered the prayers, loved them, and then they went home to reflect. They apparently got together and talked about it, and after being unable to come up with answers to their questions, walked to the Baptist Student Ministries building and interrupted the service to find answers. They didn't get a sermon about going to hell; they only had their questions answered, and with that, they knew everything they needed to know and decided they wanted to know Jesus personally. They didn't join a religion; they entered into relationship with God. It was awesome and beautiful and my faith grew tremendously.

Holy Spirit is more amazing than I had imagined or comprehended. I saw God meeting people in the place they were so I let them go, and trusted God to finish the work. In that, they had to wrestle with what they had encountered. These men found they could not explain what they had seen or heard, and went to the only place they knew to go to get answers; but they were not taught doctrine, and they gave their lives to Christ because something was clear to them - they encountered God. If I had tried to teach them and convert them or tried to get them to repent first, they would not have given their lives to Jesus because getting people to repent first rarely works. We just needed to introduce them to God's goodness and let God do the rest. Not once did we ask "Do you want to give your life to Christ?" They were the ones to ask, "What do I need to do?"

A CALL TO BE HOT

The next Sunday I preached my first sermon without notes. God told me that if I allowed Him to speak, and did not rely on notes, the entire church would commit to a new relationship with Him. As I stood up to preach at the pulpit, I had no clue what to preach or from which scripture. There was a fear building inside me, full of doubt. I was having a difficult time trusting that God would actually speak. Suddenly, however, I felt the need to look at Revelation 3. I told the church to turn there, and we learned a lot about God's desire for His people to be burning hot for Him, and not to be lukewarm. There were 72 people in our church that morning. Of the 72 there, when I gave the altar call, 72 people came forward with the desire to serve God more, to give Him more, to live for Him more, and to be "hot." So we celebrated the resurrection of our church after all, only a week later than I had hoped, and more powerfully than I had dreamed.

Within a week, I had prayed for over 900 people and 500 had entered into a relationship with Jesus. Within a month, I had seen over 1,000 people come into a relationship with Christ. Within 3 months, over 2,000 people had come to know Jesus in a very intimate way. Since then, I have experienced countless people come to Christ by simply introducing them to the love of God while displaying it with power. These testimonies and encounters, especially in the first few months after Easter 2015, have truly marked my life and identity in Christ.

One such story was David, an A/C repair man. In early May of 2015, our church's air conditioner went out. In South Texas, this is a big deal, as temperatures regularly top 100 degrees. We called for the repair, and the company sent two men, one named David. The younger guy was up on the roof, and David was inside the building. I was working in my office, but felt the urge to go talk to him, so I did. I found out David was Catholic, but was struggling with drug addiction and suicidal thoughts. He had no relationship with Jesus. I shared my testimony, even talking about how at 19 years of age, I had attempted suicide 3 times. I shared how God helped me through that difficult season of my life, and how recently He had healed me completely. David wanted what I told him about: The Peace of God, and the Love of God. So he prayed with me, and he was completely filled with peace he had never experienced before. I explained the Peace he felt was actually Jesus and His love. David was instantly, noticeably, completely different. When the younger man got down from the roof, he commented, "Man, David, what's up? You look different! Your eyes are different!" Apologetics and theology do not lead people like David to the Lord, what does is an encounter with the Person of Holy Spirit; He brings transformation.

BLUE

A month later, another A/C unit went down. I called the repairmen to come, and they sent two different men to work on it. This time, I talked to the older man, and he loved Jesus. It was great. We were just talking about all God has done for us, and then the younger guy stepped in. I'll call him Blue since what stood out to me most was the blue devil-worshipping tattoos all over him; the phrase "child of Satan" on his throat and devil horns on his forehead gave him away.

Blue interrupted with a snide, "So you're a pastor? How can you force lies on people? How can you sleep at night knowing you are lying to everyone?"

It was pretty easy to sense the hostility. Now, I had never before responded the way I did to Blue, and haven't since. What came out of my mouth still shocks me, "What did God do to you that is making you hate Him so much?" It was very aggressive.

Without wasting a second, Blue responded, "He killed my parents when I was 5 and my grandparents when I was 18."

By now, I knew better than to think God killed his family. I had read John 10:10. Jesus gives life. Satan kills. God only gives perfect gifts. I spent the next 15 minutes talking with Blue about why he blamed God, why it was wrong to blame Him, and why he was loved by God.

Blue replied, "But every single decision I have made in the past 15 years was to make God mad. I have deliberately tried to hate Him most of my life."

I understood, and insisted that despite his best efforts, Blue had not pushed God away.

"You mean, all I have to do is say I'm sorry and God will forgive me?" he wondered.

"You don't even need to say you're sorry. He already knows." My reply was shocking to me, what came out of my mouth contradicted everything I had been taught, which was "repent first", "ask for forgiveness". The reason I know now that my reply was the heart of God, is because in that instant, Blue fell to his knees, in the front of our sanctuary stage and he said only one thing, "Thank you Father." Tears streamed down Blue's tattooed face, his hands over his heart. He worshipped the God of Love and forgiveness. His older co-worker and I joined in, praising our Heavenly Father for loving us.

STILL ON FIRE

Early on after I woke up from my spiritual coma, a few friends and family noticed my passion. They all commended me, and then they would always make a comment like, "Enjoy it while it lasts. The pendulum always swings hard." I knew what they meant. That was exactly what my old life looked like. I would get on fire, but then I would backslide. I heard it a few times, to be certain. I remember a nurse I prayed for said to me, "Oh honey, give it two years and we will see where you are." If you ask anyone, who has known me since April 2015, about me, I promise you will hear something like this, "Oh, he's worse now than he was then!" This means I am more on fire for Jesus today than ever.

No one was concerned for my faith in May of 2015. No one had left the church because I had lost my mind. No one was questioning my sanity. Some have left since then because I have grown to know things that go beyond what they can accept. So I am more radical today than I was yesterday. I want to be more radical tomorrow than I am today. The more I pursue Jesus, the more radical I become, and that excites me.

Chapter 3

Healing

"If God healed me and answers prayers, what else don't I know about?" Pursuing an answer to this question was the next step in my growth. There was a single question that drove me: What else have I not been taught about God? In other words, what is the next thing I need to learn about in my new-found relationship with my loving, Heavenly Father? During those first 3 days of praying for people, I just prayed for God to meet peoples' needs. But with this new pursuit into freedom, I began to specifically go out to pray for healing.

I began to pray for people daily. I went across the street to the football stadium, where they were having Spring Football practice. This is always a tough time for football players, because kids are desperate to make the team, to impress coaches, and to get as much playing time as possible in an attempt to get on the field in the Fall, when the real season is going on. Since kids have this attitude and desperation, there tends to be more injuries in the Spring. I would sit in the stands during practice and make notes of which kids got hurt, and then after practice I would pray for them. One afternoon, after practice, I prayed for over 30 guys as they left the training room with ice packs and wraps, before they could get into the locker room. The first guy I prayed for was a Tight End, I'll call Joe. Joe had come to church a few times, and recognized me. I asked him what was wrong with him, and he showed me the ice pack on his thigh.

"I tore my quad. Looks like I'm done. My career is probably over."

I replied, "Nah, man. I'm going to pray for you, and God is going to heal you so you can practice tomorrow."

He denied it, taking off the ice pack and wrap to show me a hole in his thigh big enough for me to put my fist inside. I have to admit, I was pretty worried, but I knew one thing: my God did the impossible when He healed me. He will do it again for Joe. So I told him to close his eyes, and to put the ice pack over the hole. Then I prayed, "Father, I thank you that you love Joe. Heal his thigh in Jesus name, so that he knows you love him and want a relationship with him. Amen." Joe opened his eyes, and then at my request, removed the ice pack. There was no hole. I told him to stretch the muscle, and so he did. There was no soreness, no stiffness, and no sign of an injury. The next day, Joe practiced without pain.

The last guy I prayed for in that line of 30 was a guy I will call Tank. He was a big guy, and at first appearance, I was scared to talk to him. He had an ice bag on his left foot. Upon talking to him, I found out he had a torn ligament on his big toe, which means he could not put any weight on it without extreme pain. I have had this injury before, and I can attest it was one of the most painful injuries of my life. Tank was not a believer, and he wanted nothing to do with the name of Jesus. At first, he would not let me pray for him. After I explained I would not hurt him, that I wasn't trying to force Jesus on him, but I simply wanted him to be healthy so he could still play,

Tank allowed me to pray. "Jesus, I thank you for loving Tank. Toe, I command you be healed in Jesus name, so that Tank can practice and play without pain, and so he knows that Jesus loves him, and wants a relationship with him." I asked him to check it; he winced and said it was no better. I tried to pray again, but he wouldn't let me. He got up and limped quickly into the locker room. Some of the guys came outside and thanked me for praying, they were very excited about being healed. Then Tank stepped out of the locker room...without a limp. I watched closely as he was laughing and joking with some of his teammates. Suddenly, he remembered me, and turned to see if I was watching him. As soon as he saw me, he began limping again. He never missed a play the rest of the week, and he played the entire game that Saturday, pain free. I still laugh when I remember Tank.

LESS "SUCCESS"

I started praying everywhere I went. I would go to Hobby Lobby or Home Depot and pray for everyone inside and outside. I would go to Dairy Queen to pray for anyone. One June day, in Dairy Queen, I found a woman with a back brace. She was in her late 80s, and I could tell without the brace, she had no ability to stand up. Her spine was in horrible shape. This was the biggest prayer request I had yet to pray for. I went up to her and asked if I could pray. After a wonderful conversation, she allowed me to pray. She wasn't totally healed, but felt stronger. This was the first time I prayed for someone and they were not completely healed. After that encounter, I noticed something I did not like. The more I prayed, the less successful I became. I was getting more and more confused. I began researching different healing teachings trying to figure out what I was doing wrong. I listened to teachings from Todd White,

Dan Mohler, and Robby Dawkins. I learned a lot from these men, but still I was slowly becoming more and more unsuccessful. I went to a conference where Todd White was speaking, and tried to learn more about healing. After a few months of searching, I made a decision to change our church service schedule. Wednesday nights were to be for prayer thinking that I needed to pray more to overcome this hurdle.

I was determined to see healing all the time, and I was not about to give up. I had tasted and seen that the Lord was good, and I knew He wanted to use me and our church to heal people. It didn't matter that I was getting more and more unsuccessful, I had to keep trying. What I found was the more miracles I saw, the more dependent on my experience I became. The more dependent on my experience, the less successful I was. For example, I had seen a leg grow out – my own leg. So when I prayed for someone with the same problem, I was thinking, "Oh this will be easy, I've already done this." Only thing is, that was not faith in God, but faith in my experience.

One morning, on my drive to Kingsville, I decided to cry out to God and ask Him why I was seeing less and less happen. His response still humbles me to this day. "You have forgotten about My love." God speaks to me in short, simple sentences. The impacts of His messages are always huge and powerful. In His simple sentence I knew what He meant. I was focused on my experience, as well as my prayer. It had become all about my technique. I was praying with an attitude of God wants to heal them, but wants me to do it. It was all about me, my prayer, my technique, and making another testimony. I was being selfish. *But the Kingdom of God is like a farmer who scatters seed. While he lays in his bed and sleeps, the garden grows* (Mark 4:26-29). It's not the kingdom of Jeff. It is the Kingdom of God. It's about His love for each person. It's about people being reconciled to their loving Father. It's about Jesus' sacrifice. Once I learned this, I have never forgotten it. It has been over 4 years since God corrected my selfishness, and since that day I have seen more and more healed. LOVE, LOVE, LOVE. My percentages are high today, but still are not 100%. There are some things I have not ever seen happen. There are things I am seeking God to see. For me, that means I have growth potential. It isn't a bad thing. Robby Dawkins told me once, if you see healings 100% of the times you pray for people, it's because you aren't taking enough risk. We need to go after the impossible. We need to pursue greater miracles. Failure isn't something I feel condemned about; it just means I need to keep growing in the Lord. Colossians 3:10 says we have taken off the old self and its practices *"and have put on the new self, which is being renewed in knowledge in the image of its Creator."*(NIV) In Philippians 3:10, Paul writes, *"That I may know him, and the power of his resurrection, and the fellowship of his sufferings, being made conformable unto his death;"* (KJV) I need to know God, and I need to be renewed in knowledge. If I am not seeing a prayer answered, then I just need to grow from faith to faith. It gives me reason to read more of His Word, to get on my knees and talk to Him, to get on my face and worship my God.

SOZO

As I have grown in the Christian mandate to heal, I have learned about SOZO. Sozo is a Greek word found in the New Testament that we translate as "saved". In John 3:17 Jesus uses the word sozo. But sozo is a very complicated word with many different meanings. So "saved" doesn't just mean to be saved. It means saved, healed, delivered, protected, and preserved, just to name a few. The reason this is important to discuss is because in my past, I thought "saved" was referring to Heaven. We are saved for Heaven, but we are not healed for Heaven, nor are we delivered, protected, or preserved for Heaven. In Heaven, those things are a given. Therefore those are for life *now*. 2 Corinthians 6:2 says, "...*Look, now is the acceptable time; now is the day of salvation.*" (HCSB) Here, the Greek does not say sozo, but says soterias, which still means deliverance, preservation, salvation, and healing. We cannot pick and choose which English word we put there. It has to say all those things, if it means all those things. Healing is important to God. Acts 10:38 says, "*how God anointed Jesus of Nazareth with the Holy Spirit and power, and how he went around doing good and healing all who were under the power of the devil, because God was with him.*" (NIV) Jesus healed all. So I have had to ask myself, "If Jesus healed all, and I am supposed to do what Jesus did, do I need to heal all?" I believe the answer is yes. As soon as I was healed, I heard God say, "Freely I have given you, now freely give." It was all I needed.

I have already told you the story of Ahmed. This was the critical moment of my walk. Without going out to the public and praying for people I do not grow. Praying for people shows me where I am at. I know whether I have faith or not because of the results I see. In Matthew 17, Luke 9, and Mark 9, we have the only story in the bible where someone prays and nothing happens. In that story, the disciples pray for a boy who has an unclean spirit, but nothing materializes. When Jesus gets there, He saves the boy. The disciples had previous experience with demons, so they were puzzled when they didn't see breakthrough, so they asked Jesus why nothing happened when they prayed. Most of this part of the story is in all three books, but Jesus' answer is different in Matthew and Mark. I believe it is because both are true. In Matthew, Jesus answered, "because of your unbelief..." In Mark, Jesus said, "this only comes from prayer and fasting." I believe we gain more faith from prayer and fasting. I believe some things only happen when we are in deep prayer and fasting. Why? Why is prayer and fasting so important to faith? I believe it boils down to another question: What is God's purpose for prayer and for fasting?

FASTING

Bryan Schwartz said in Adventures with God, that prayer and fasting are designed to develop intimacy with God. I love the passage found in Isaiah 58:5-7.

"Is this the kind of fast I have chosen, only a day for people to humble themselves? Is it only for bowing one's head like a reed and for lying in sackcloth and ashes? Is that what you call a fast, a day acceptable to the LORD? "Is not this the kind of fasting I have chosen: to loose the chains of injustice and untie the cords of the yoke, to set the oppressed free and break every yoke? Is it not to share your food with the hungry and to provide the poor wanderer with shelter— when you see the naked, to clothe them, and not to turn away from your own flesh and blood? (NIV)

There is purpose in prayer and fasting. Intimacy with God is what He desires. The more intimate I am with Him, the better I know Him. The better I know Him, the more I want to serve Him. The more I serve Him, from that place of intimacy, the more I will see His will be done on earth as it is in Heaven. The purposes of prayer and fasting are to set the oppressed free and to break every yoke of bondage. This is where healing, deliverance, salvation, and preservation come in. I fast fairly often. I don't have a set schedule, but it is close to one day each week. Sometimes I fast for six or seven days in a row, and other times I fast for two or three days. I let God tell me when and for how long. I recently did a 60 day fast where I ate one meal every three days. The amount of miracles I saw during a five day stretch of that fast was incredible. I saw things I never dreamed, such as bones move under my hand and supernaturally line up before all the pain disappeared. I even felt heat and energy surge through my body and enter the person I was praying for. I saw a man get new lungs, after being lifted off the ground and falling backwards about 6 feet...

OPEN THY MOUTH WIDE

He was 84 years old and needed a double lung transplant. I was about 14 feet away from him and there was no way to reach him, as I was at a conference with over 2,000 people helping with the ministry time, laying hands on and praying for people and the crowd was just too thick. I didn't know him, and actually, I never met him. There was a younger man (about 60 years old) who was with him. I heard God tell me He was going to heal "Richard", even though I had yet to know what was wrong. Because I could not reach Richard, I motioned to the younger man to get behind him and catch him, in case he was slain in the spirit. The younger man moved back behind him, and when he was ready, I said over the crowd, "Fire of Heaven fall on Richard! I command new lungs in Jesus' name!" Now, I didn't know about his lungs. I had not heard from God that Richard was going to have his lungs healed. And the only reason I knew his name was because God told me. It wasn't until I began to speak that it came out of my mouth. There wasn't a thought at all about lungs. My mouth simply said it, just as it says in Psalm 81:10, *"I am the LORD thy God, which brought thee out of the land of Egypt: open thy mouth wide, and I will fill it."* (KJV) I opened my mouth and God filled it with a prayer. When I said the prayer, and again all I said was fire fall and new lungs, Richard immediately left the ground, went up about six inches off the ground and knocked the younger man down, as he flew backwards. When I saw this, I freaked because I have never seen anything like that in my life. Richard was lying on top of the younger man. I began to force myself through the crowd to find out what happened. Richard had his eyes closed the entire time. He did not know I was going to pray for him. He was simply worshipping God. When I got to them, the younger man was wiggling his way out from underneath Richard. I asked him what happened. He stated, "This is my father. He is 84 and needs a double lung transplant." I told him what I prayed and then asked if there was any way we could find out what happened. He showed me on Richard's wrist was an oxygen meter. I told the son I believed his dad was healed. When he looked at the meter it said 100%. His son began to cry, so I asked him what it normally says. "The best I have ever seen is 75%, but it is typically around 25%."

Right after that, I prayed for a man with a tumor attached to his stomach. It was visible, as it was sticking out under his rib cage. I prayed, "Tumor I curse you and command you to dissolve right now. I command complete healing in Jesus' name." My hand was on the tumor, and it disappeared before I could finish the prayer. He checked it, but could not find it either. Person after person, I saw so many healings that day. God is amazing. This was in the middle of my fast, day 21. For the next 5 days I continued to see miraculous healings. Fasting has serious effect on our growth and our faith.

HOLY SPIRIT HEALS

I have had many Christians who do not believe in healing the way I do ask me "So do you heal people?" Healing is possible only through Holy Spirit. He moves through us. I have never healed anyone. My words have never healed anyone. My faith, when aligned with His Will, gives power to the prayer that brings healing. As James wrote in the 5th chapter of his letter, verses 15 and 16,

"And the prayer offered in faith will make the sick person well; the Lord will raise them up. If they have sinned, they will be forgiven. Therefore confess your sins to each other and pray for each other so that you may be healed. The prayer of a righteous person is powerful and effective." (NIV)

Even Jesus, in John 14:10, said, *"Don't you believe that I am in the Father, and that the Father is in me? The words I say to you are not just my own. Rather, it is the Father living in me, who is doing the work."* We have a scripture where Jesus said He didn't heal with His prayers! He actually says here that when He prays, His Father, The Father, does the work. This is why I say healing is possible only through Holy Spirit. We serve a God who has set it up for us to be a part of His Kingdom. As for more understanding about what is really happening, let's examine more scripture. In Genesis, God formed man out of dust, and woman was made from man. Therefore both are made of dust. Our bodies are made of dust. God gave Adam authority over all the earth in Chapter 1. When we are justified, we are reset to before we ever sinned, so we are reset to what Adam had. If he had dominion over all creation, we do too. So we are simply taking back authority from the devil. We are simply getting aligned with God and allowing God to move through us to do His will, which is to do good and to heal all.

I have encountered people who have faith, but not in God alone. For example, I heard a teenage girl say she believed God was going to heal a woman (which she had never seen before) because a camera was recording her, trying to document the miracle. She was certain that God would heal the woman, not because of God, but because God would be compelled by the camera. I have seen people pray with faith in the situation, as if God would be motivated by the circumstances in a moment.

What about God's will? What about His love for the person? We must not lose focus on His love for people. We can never lose sight of loving others with His love, since "we love because He first loved us." "Love covers a multitude of sins." I think John and Peter learned from Jesus, don't you? Is it any wonder, then, that they taught similar points? In John 14:12 John wrote that Jesus said, *"whoever believes in me, they will do greater things than what I have been doing..."* and then in 14:15, *"If you love me, keep my commands."* The greater things Jesus referred to are completely connected to LOVE. Both John and Peter, in their letters (1 John 4, 1 Peter 4) they were referring to loving people. Why? Simply put, it is because God loves people, and He wants us to as well. He doesn't heal people because of an anointing. He doesn't heal because someone is filming it. He doesn't heal because His reputation is on the line. God heals because of LOVE. Like I wrote earlier, I went from seeing 10 healings a day, to maybe 1 a week, but when I prayed and asked God why, His reply was about His Love. It's who He is. It's not what He does. His identity is goodness and love, and therefore His fruit is good things and love.

WHEN ATHEISTS PRAY

I have also seen healing come without faith. I have encountered groups of atheists on a few occasions. Since they are so against God, I often encourage them to pray for each other to the God they don't believe in. For example, "Kristina" had a severely sprained ankle and was using crutches. I approached her and her friends at a store, with the intention of praying for her healing. However, I was met with extreme hostility and proclamations of my stupidity for believing in God. So I simply said, "Okay, let me prove to you that God exists. I will have one of you pray for Kristina and I won't actually pray, so that you know it isn't me, and God will heal her." They were intrigued and actually really confident that they were going to "take down a pastor." So I told one girl that I would simply lead her in a prayer and that she could repeat after me, because she didn't know how to pray. She agreed and Kristina was healed instantly. Because of this, I was able to explain that God is, in fact, real, and that He wanted a relationship with them. They didn't even discuss it, the whole group wanted to know God. An atheist prayed for another atheist to be healed, and God introduced Himself to them. Where was the faith in that? Who had the faith? Sometimes, God just wants people to know He loves them.

YOU NEVER KNOW WHO'S WATCHING

I went to a Dairy Queen for lunch one day, reluctantly. You see, I didn't want to go to Dairy Queen that day for lunch. I had other plans. I drove 5 miles and passed up 17 other restaurants to get there, and the whole time I was driving wondering where God was taking me. It was very crowded and loud. I ordered my food and sat down at a small table while I waited for my food to come. Suddenly, I realized the place was quiet. I looked up and saw that the restaurant was empty except for one old man on the other side of the room, and the three employees. Two of the employees took an opportunity to rest and sit down after an obvious rush had just ended.

My food came, and I began to eat when I overheard the two women talking, "At my next break, I am going to go to the back and cry." The other lady responded, "It hurts that bad?"

I suddenly knew why I was there and why the room had emptied so quickly. This was a divine appointment. I finished eating because, I don't know about you but I get really nervous approaching strangers to pray for them. If I have any excuse, I typically get too nervous and use my nerves as an excuse to back out of talking to strangers. As I finished eating the woman in pain was standing by the trash, so it was a perfect opportunity for me to overcome my fears.

As I took my trash to throw it away I approached her, "Excuse me, I overheard you saying earlier that you are hurting. Is it your back?"

She said it was her back and that she was in terrible pain.

I added, "Ma'am, I am a Christian and I believe God sent me here to pray for you. I believe He wants to heal you because He wants a relationship with you."

She replied, "I am a Christian, and I would love for God to heal me. You really think He will?"

"Yes ma'am, He will heal you right now if you let me pray," I answered. So I began to pray. I didn't touch her, because I didn't want to intrude, but my right hand was hovering less than an inch from her lower back. I prayed for her, and her pain went from a 10 to a 7. I prayed again, it went to a 4. With the third prayer the pain went to a 1.

She ran out of time, and told me I had to stop because she had to get back to work. I stopped, and we both turned to walk away when all of a sudden she turned back to me and said, "Wait! What did you just do? All the pain and stiffness just left! It's all gone!"

I just smiled, as she hugged me, and told her, "I didn't do anything but pray. God healed you."

She went back to work and the other ladies asked her if she really got healed, and she yelled in excitement, "Yes! All the pain is gone!" I grabbed my cup of sweet tea and walked out the door.

As I got in my car, I saw the only other patron, the old man, running out of the restaurant waving his hands at me, so I rolled down my window. He stuck his hand in my car and said,

"Young man, I am a pastor and I believe in Holy Spirit. I have believed in healing and seen it in church my entire life, but I have never prayed for someone in public. Thank you for being an imitator of Jesus and doing what He did. God just used you to change me. I will do this, just like you did. Thank you so much!" It was there in the car that I realized God took me there to not only pray for the woman, but to ignite an older pastor to do more than he was. God truly loves it when we pray for people, when we let Him heal through us.

KEEP PRESSING IN

I failed quite a few times when praying for healing. There was a 4 month period where I didn't see a single person get healed from prayer. Today, I would say I see about 85% get healed. I recently prayed for a man with cancer. He had a tumor attached to his intestines. The tumor was found to have died shortly after the prayer, and the intestines were fixed miraculously. On the same day I received the news about that man, I found out another woman I prayed for a few weeks prior with a tumor passed away. I don't know why some get healed, and some don't. What I do know is Jesus told us to heal the sick.

I have heard Robby Dawkins say multiple times, "I don't know if Healing is a gift. If you don't think it's your gift, then try obedience." Jesus told his followers in Matthew 10 and Luke 10 when sending out the 70/72, "Heal the sick, raise the dead, cleanse the lepers, and cast out demons. Freely you have received, freely give." Jesus told them to heal the sick, period. Then he told them in the Great Commission to go make disciples of the nations, teaching all He had commanded of them. So then, I am a disciple. And I have been included in the instructions to heal the sick. He didn't tell me to be concerned with why some don't get healed. He told me to heal sick and injured people. We must keep pressing in. Whether you are three years old, or 93 years old God wants to use you.

I have witnessed countless healings in the short time since I was set free from religion and its traditional thinking, and learned God heals. I have seen 18 people get out of wheel chairs and take their first steps (back to their vehicles as I followed, carrying their wheelchairs). It doesn't happen every time, however. Often, it takes multiple prayers, but if Jesus needed to pray two times for a man, then I guess it is ok for me to, as well. There have been many cases when I have prayed for someone where the pain level, mobility, or inflammation, slowly went down on a scale of 1-10. My friend teaches to use a scale to measure the effectiveness, for helping to discern what is needed. When I approach someone for prayer, I ask them to check the pain level and then we call that pain a 10. Then, I pray. After the prayer, I ask them to check and see the pain level. This is where the scale comes in handy. Most of the time the pain level drops from a 10 to an 8 (for example), so that means there is improvement, but not total healing. This is a clue to pray again, which, most of the time the pain drops to maybe a 4. Sometimes it is completely healed, sometimes it stays at an 8. I have learned a lot about healing and the enemy because of these results.

"PRAY LIKE A CHILD"

When praying for healing, a single prayer may be all that is needed, but sometimes it can take multiple prayers. Just the other day, we had a few people come up to the front of the church for prayer with knee pains after our church service. One guy had a giant swollen knot on the back of his knee. As I prayed, the knot shrunk in half. Then it shrunk some more, but the pain hadn't decreased. So before I prayed a third time, I felt

God tell me to "pray like a little child." So I prayed, "Owie, be gone. Go away!" At that, the pain left and the swelling left. The next person in line had come to me before with knee problems. She said, "You prayed for my knee about 4 months ago, and I felt electricity run down my leg and has been great ever since, but then about 2 weeks ago a different pain started." Any time we see something go away and come back, this tells us there is spiritual opposition from the enemy (I address this further in the chapter on spiritual warfare). So I bound the spirit – for her it was a tormenting spirit (Matthew 4:24) - that was causing the pain, and removed it.

I did this by recognizing Jesus paid for her need to be healed and understanding my faith. I established my authority over the spirit so it had to do what I said, because we have been given authority over the earth and everything in it. *"The highest heavens belong to the Lord, but the earth He has given to the control of man."* (Psalm 115:16) When we announce our faith and operate from it, the enemy has no choice but to obey. Immediately, the pain in her knee dropped from a 10 to a 4. I prayed again, and it stayed at a 4. I was about to pray a third time, when I felt there was a crick inside her knee. I don't really know how I felt it or knew it was there, but I did. I often feel things before or during a time of praying for people and I just stay sensitive in the moment allowing myself to be led by Holy Spirit; sometimes it's a gut feeling, other times a thought enters my mind and I just know. There are countless ways God can speak to us when we are inviting Him in to set people free. I commanded the crick to leave. It left immediately and the pain dropped to a 1. I was going to pray a fourth time, but then I felt God tell me to "Have her sing to me." So I told her to sing. I expected her to sing a song from the radio or something like that, but she just started making something up. It was great! Then God directed me to have her sing two things: "Thank

You Lord that You love me." And "Thank You Lord that Your love has healed me." As soon as she sang those lines, she was completely healed. God wants to heal us.

I think even more than that, God wants us to know He loves us. The more I focus on His love for the person, the more often I see healings. Sometimes we pray for symptoms, and sometimes we realize there are spiritual things involved and remove the spirit as Jesus did in Mark 1 and Matthew 8 when he removed the spirits and people were healed.

FORGIVENESS, A GATE TO HEALING

Sometimes, there are internal reasons for healing. One day, during our Saturday school of ministry, a man named Charles came in because he needed healing in his knee. I had some of the students pray for it, for practice. The first guy to pray was excited to try, he ran across the room and he prayed with command and compassion, which are both key to healing. Charles wasn't really in pain, he just had no strength in his knee after having surgery a few times. He had an awful limp, and his leg would tremble constantly. So the student prayed, and the pain Charles did have left his knee. It was still shaking and weak, so I asked someone else to pray, and they did. There was not much change, so I prayed. While I was praying, I heard the word "forgiveness," so I stopped praying. Hearing this word pop up in my mind, informed me he needed to forgive some-body; I knew healing would not come until he forgave.

I waited for the other students who wanted a chance to pray to finish, then I asked him to come back to the front of the room where I was standing. He hobbled over, almost at the point of giving up. I was using this opportunity to teach the class. I prayed again, but this time I didn't pray for healing. I prayed for forgiveness and confession. "Father, I thank you that you love this man, and I pray a spirit of forgiveness would go into him so that he would forgive anyone who has hurt him and a spirit of confession would pour out of him so he would confess anything that would hold back his healing, amen." The reason I prayed for forgiveness and confession is found in scripture. First, I was thinking of James 5:13-16. In that passage, James wrote people who want healing sometimes need to confess their sins to each other. It seems like confession and healing can be an exchange, just like praise and despair can be exchanged as mentioned in Isaiah 61. My prayer for this guy with the bad knee was new for me. As soon as I prayed those words, I was expecting Charles to confess that he did not want to forgive someone, and so I waited for him to say something. He looked around the room, and asked me, "Is there somewhere you and I can talk?"

I took him to another room and he confessed a lot of things from the last five to ten years of his life choices. As soon as he finished confessing them, I forgave him, and then told him to stand up. He started to walk across the room. Within a few seconds, he was running down the hall in tears. We all worshipped God with him. His knee was healed, not because of a prayer, but because he confessed. He needed healing on the inside much more than his knee. When he got healing inside of him, the outer healing was a given. Charles' story revealed to me if someone holds on to guilt and shame this keeps them from not letting go of their past and forgiving (mainly themselves). Then many times, the thing they are wanting to happen will not happen. God wants to heal the spiritual side and forgiveness can be the key to unlock the healing. He wants all His children to live completely free and holding onto resentment can often block the healing.

John 20:22-23 talks about something Jesus told his disciples. His quote says, "*Receive Holy Spirit. If you forgive anyone their sins, they are forgiven...*"For a long time I couldn't understand why these two sentences were beside each other because they don't really seem to relate. Receive Holy Spirit sounds great. Forgive other's sins, and they will be forgiven sounds like a completely different subject, unless forgiveness allows you to receive Holy Spirit, then they make sense. I personally find it interesting the bible mentions when Jesus would encounter people and before many people were healed, Jesus forgave them of their sins. I know He is the Messiah, so He should do that, but then He told the disciples to do it too. In my prayer for Charles, I prayed for forgiveness because I heard "unforgiveness", remembered the James 5 scripture, and tested it out. I believe if I can forgive someone, then God forgives them. I do not believe I have the power to erase their sins, but if I can look past their sins, if I can forget their sins, if I can love them despite their sins, then I know God does. Scriptures say He does.

God looks past every horrible decision I have ever made and He does this every second of my life, and doesn't hold my sins against me (Hebrews 8:12). I have been forgiven. I must forgive others too, for me and for them. Confession is really important because it allows me to forgive myself. I confess regularly. My wife knows my past. I told her everything I've ever done that haunted me, and I have told her multiple times. My church knows my past. I have confessed from the pulpit. I don't believe in secrets when it comes to sin. I expose my dark to the light because true inner healing is sometimes more important than the physical healing. I say "true" because I don't exactly believe in the traditional inner healing teachings; those take steps and are slow in bringing freedom, and often don't actually bring freedom but creates a to-do list and masks the shame with obedience, trading one slavery-mentality for another. My depression and bipolar disorder didn't go away because of counseling or inner healing methods. Those things taught me how to manage my depression and crazy mood swings. What healed me was having a personal revelation of what Jesus did for me on the cross. My fear, anger, wrath, jealousy, depression, and frustrations left the moment I embraced the fact that Jesus really loves me, and that He died for me to be justified. Jesus did not die for you to manage your symptoms and find out which door you opened. He wants to present you with a new door to walk through.

The moment I understood justification, which means I have been reset – every curse, attack of the enemy, "open door" that can be focused on, is now no longer relevant, because I have been reset and they no longer apply when I believe and accept Jesus' work on the cross. Inner healing makes you more aware of who you were rather than who Jesus has died for you to become. Inner healing works, but it takes a lot longer than is necessary and doesn't always set us totally free. Believing in inner healing runs a risk of missing the purpose of the cross: to set you free. The blood of Jesus is the most powerful, most valuable offering given to me and I choose to receive it. It is how I was set free, and have been free ever since. This is "true inner healing." I also want to take a moment to say that I have a few friends who have been truly helped through the process of inner healing, but all of them are people who understand the cross, the power of Holy Spirit, and know not to focus on the things of the soul more than the spirit. What do you choose to believe about what the cross fully did for you?

THERE'S NO METHOD

Another teaching I have found in the more charismatic circles is the requirement of laying on of hands. It is biblical, no doubt. James 5 tells us that the elders of the church are to lay hands on the sick person and pray. However, I do not think it is always necessary and can easily become another doctrine or tradition. A few months ago, one of the members of my church was complaining about her eyesight and how it had gotten really blurry. There was a group of people standing around, and typically I would use that opportunity to have one of them pray. This time, I felt I needed to do something else. The person with the bad eyes was formerly of a very charismatic church that taught you must lay hands. One of the other people there also believed that. Suddenly, I felt the need to just move my hand in front of her eyes, as if she would be healed without a touch or even a word being spoken. I put my hand in front of her eyes and acted like I grabbed something and pulled it off. She blinked and looked around and responded with, "No way! My eyes are clear!"

I think sometimes, God just wants us to get out of the box and see that He does not fit inside. It is as if He does not want us following a method, but being more like flowing water, moving where it is easiest to go. Often, healing comes when we are outside the standard ways that are taught. What I know is this: God deserves honor, glory, and recognition. "In Jesus name" isn't an abra cadabra saying. When I say it, I truly mean to acknowledge Jesus. Occasionally I say "for the Glory of God" to make sure the person I am praying for understands it is all for God's glory and praise. All of this to say God does not heal in just one way, He moves based off of what is really needed: sometimes it can take laying on of hands, or takes anointing oil, or confession of sins or offenses, or praying like a child, praying with absolute authority, or healing a heart, or an emotional wound from 20 years ago, or simply just listening to the person. If I can hear from Holy Spirit what God is actually wanting to heal, then the thing they came for gets healed in the moment.

I mentioned there are some things I have not yet seen get healed. I have only recently seen a blind eye open. The reality is the first time I saw it the man had no left eye. I prayed the first time, he opened his eyelid and there was half of an eye, (which looked as strange as it sounds), the second time I prayed he had an entire eye but it was completely white (it was hard to stay calm and not freak out at this point), by the third time I prayed he had a whole eye, a rich brown iris right there where it should be and the most beautiful part is the man could see! At that point I had prayed for people over 4 years and prayed for multiple blind eyes to open and never saw it until then. However, I have a student who had only been a believer for a year and I find it funny because I have taught him to pray and to pursue healings, and he got to see a blind eye get opened before I did. I have seen bad eyes get better a few times, though, and I have seen blind eyes healed when a group of us pray. I have not seen a limb grow out. We have a boy at our church that I have prayed for a few times, who only has half of an arm. His dad and I are pursuing his healing. I truly believe one day it will grow out. On the flip side, I have seen deaf ears opened. I have seen stroke victims completely restored. I have seen countless legs grow out. I have seen people get out of wheel chairs. I have seen broken bones shift and be healed. I have felt spines align. I have watched tumors dissolve, and skin cancers literally fall off of people. It always happens because of God's love for the person. Our job is to love the person, to see them through God's eyes, and to get Heaven on earth – into them. Whether it's a broken leg, cancer, or a tummy ache, Jesus wants to heal the person. The best part about this is He wants to use us!

WHAT'S THE WORST THAT CAN HAPPEN?

The most interesting thing I learned about healing ministry is the reaction that comes when healing doesn't happen. That used to be my biggest fear and reason to not pray. What I discovered is when you love on a person, even when healing does not come, they are typically so moved by the compassion and faith they still give their life to Jesus. People want to know God. Atheists, Hindus, Muslims, it doesn't matter what their background. They are so amazed by the fact that I believe in my God so much to pray to Him for healing, that they do not seem to mind when healing doesn't happen. They usually say a statement that at least sounds something like this, "Wow, you really believe in your God. I have never seen someone that believes like you. You're not a hypocrite. Most people don't actually believe anything because they never do anything, but you did. Why are you different? How did you become like this? What church do you go to? I wish I could believe in God like you do." From there, it is pretty simple to lead someone to a relationship with Christ. I am always humbled by this situation. What seems like the worst thing that could happen is sometimes what God uses to draw people to Him.

"I DON'T BELONG IN THIS GROUP"

I used to meet with a group of pastors from my denominational background. There were seven of us who met the first Monday of every month and I enjoyed meeting with them. Most of us were in our first three years of being a pastor, so it really helped to talk about situations and to learn from each other. However, about the time of my healing (which I call an awakening from my spiritual coma), I noticed the amount of judging we did of other denominations. Allow me to repeat some of my past. I was raised Baptist, and I deeply agreed with everything Baptist. Even though I had gone to my now-wife's Pentecostal church, I completely opposed their practices and beliefs that were different than mine. I, in no way, ever weakened in my stance to anything I ever heard that was contrary to my upbringing. It was the same while I was helping out at the small Methodist church for a year. I actually tried to convince them of all I knew to be true. Part of my goal was to show them their errors and prove I was correct.

So when I joined the pastor group, I loved it because they were like me. But when I "woke up" I noticed that these men were somehow different than me. I continued to meet with the group for six months. I was amazed at how fast I changed. I barely enjoyed being around them, with all the crude jokes I used to find funny, and all the things they said about other denominations' doctrine. For those first six months, the only pastors I ever talked to were the other six men in our group. I definitely did not talk to other denominations. Once I was healed, I changed so quickly, as I quit pursuing doctrine and tradition to chase after Jesus' image. One day, these men started talking about how pathetic and false pastors are for teaching about healing, and how tragic it is to see people who believe what they teach. It was more than I could take. Each man in the group bashed healing. They laughed at the idea that God would respond to men's pleas.

"But what about Jesus' teachings in places like Luke 11, where He said "*Keep asking, Keep seeking, Keep knocking,* or that a person's persistence will move God to give a person what they need?" I thought. Then, apparently, it was my turn to join in on the mocking because they all looked at me, as if waiting for me to chime in. I was in tears. I had seen over 2,000 people accept Christ and start a relationship with a God who loves them, simply and solely because of prayers for healing in the last half year. The people I prayed for were so moved by God's love, but these godly men were making fun of people who believed God heals. I was in shock. I don't remember what all I said, but I remember one sentence, "I don't belong in this group anymore." This one statement started a conversation with them asking me questions and me answering them as best I could. I remember the first pastor getting up and leaving (he actually just walked out into the hallway, I later discovered). I remember two other pastors shortly following him, after condemning me to hell. I remember that only one pastor stayed in the room to actually ask sincere questions, he stayed in the room for 45 minutes with me. We had assumed the others had all gone home, but when we both went into the hallway, all the men were there talking. I could not shake how furious they looked, and it broke my heart. I was never invited back. I started getting phone calls soon after that meeting from many other pastors in the area to ask questions and truthfully speaking, to just belittle me. It's been more than four years since that day. What I find odd is these men detest me in a group, but if they need prayers, if they need healing, they call me. And God hasn't let them down yet.

Chapter 4

Tongues

This is probably my scariest topic. It seems that every time I mention the word "tongues" to someone, I get attacked or someone leaves the church, but it was the next thing God taught me, after healing. Healing was so easy for me, compared to tongues. May 28, 2015 was the first time I felt God encouraging me to speak in tongues. I was terrified because I had been taught against it very well. I remember being with my grandparents in Armenia in 2005, when a woman started to speak in tongues. My grandfather argued with her and broke her of it. It was an intense conversation, to be sure. As soon as she began to speak in tongues, he stopped her. I couldn't tell she was speaking in tongues since we were in Armenia and that's a pretty crazy language anyway, but he knew instantly. He told her it was demonic and not of God. He argued with her that it is just made up noises that serve no purpose. She tried to defend it, but couldn't win. Eventually, she conceded and received correction from him.

There was at least one version of tongues we did accept. During that same trip, I noticed my grandfather and one of the pastors we worked with could talk for hours without understanding each other's language. It was fascinating to watch two men talk in their own languages without an interpreter for so long, completely comprehending each other. My grandfather would just speak in English and the other man would speak in Armenian, neither having any idea how to understand the other's language, but they would truly understand each other. It was wild to witness. I was just sitting in the back seat of the car, in complete awe of what I was witnessing. When I asked my grandpa how he knew what the other man was saying, he answered, "This is real tongues Jeff. I have experienced this everywhere I have been." And I took his word for it.

"PUT YOUR HAND ON THAT MAN'S CHEST"

I was the cameraman for the mission trip to Armenia in 2005, filming everything my grandfather and his team did to create highlights when we returned home. At the end of that trip, we went to a sun worshipper's home. He was an elderly man, and many of his family members were interested in learning more about Jesus. He had many questions, but as my grandfather or the pastor would try to answer him, he would completely interrupt them. This happened for about two hours. Every time someone would try to read scripture, it was like he didn't want to hear it. I began to pray and ask God why or how this was even possible. "How can this man know they are quoting scripture?" I suddenly felt like I needed to walk across the room and place my hand on this man's chest. It was an intense desire, but consequentially a huge fear also arose. The problem was this man was a sun worshipper. In his house, he had a bedroom fully furnished for Satan. Yes, you read that correctly: the Yezidi people actually have a bedroom set aside just in case Satan decides to visit. When they cook food, they serve a plate and leave it in the room in case Satan is hungry; this is actually standard practice for Yezidi Kurds. They dedicate the best room in the house for the devil. It has the best silk sheets, candles, and everything else possible so that when he comes, he doesn't attack them or kill anyone. I was terrified to touch this man. The desire, however, did not lessen so I knew I had to do something. I called my grandmother over to where I was sitting, and told her I thought God was telling me that she should put her hand on the man's chest. (I know, that isn't what God said to me, but I was just that terrified). She saw right through me, and clearly said if God told me to do something, I better do it. So I got up, gave her the camera, walked right up to the man, and put my hand on his chest.

I can still feel the fear when I remember the scene. Here I was 22 years old, walking up to a Sun-worshipping, devil-catering man, all because I had a feeling that if I put my hand on his chest, the demons, which I could literally see with my eyes, above his body, would leave so somehow God would move through my action and help us so we could finally share the gospel with this man and his entire family. As I walked across the room, my grandmother filming behind me, my grandfather looking in bewilderment as I passed his seat, I was terrified. I looked up at the demons, and they were looking right at me. Fearful thoughts flooded my mind as I walked, wondering what I was going to do once my hand was on his chest. I had no grid for this experience, and was clueless what would happen. As soon as I put my hand on his chest, I immediately felt as if God opened up Heaven and came down on top of my head. I felt something like an intense power come down and then go through my body and it went out through my hand, and pinned the man against the wall. He looked at me in awe. I began to speak to him, telling him about my God. He talked to me. He suddenly was speaking perfect English! The man and I didn't need the translator to talk. The translator was in shock, as she was an atheist. I was in shock. The man was in shock. My grandparents were in shock. The pastor was in shock. I explained to this man the power we were both feeling was the presence of God, and that if he would receive it, God would heal him. I urged him to open up his heart. He replied, "I don't want to." As soon as he said those words, the power left us. I said one last thing to him, which was, "Well there is nothing more I can do for you," and when I did, he turned to the translator and asked her what I said. Unbeknownst to me, my grandmother had filmed the entire conversation. In the film, I speak English, and he speaks Yezidi. He heard me speak Yezidi, and I heard him speaking perfect English. I saw him speak in English. The translator gave her life to Jesus after we left the house because of the encounter. I don't know if the man ever accepted Jesus, but I watched as his entire family did that day and I recently found out his son became a pastor.

HOLY SPIRIT: THE BEST TRANSLATOR

Because of these two experiences, these were the two types of tongues I believed in: 1. hearing a language you don't speak, but still understanding it; 2. hearing someone speak a different language than they actually are just like in the book of Acts 2:5-12. I have since experienced both of these types, the first one happens every time I go to another country. Whether it is Israel, Laos, Philippines, Kenya, or Mexico, I have experienced talking to people in English while they all speak their language. It always shocks me that it actually works because I think it's crazy. People speaking a language I do not know, and yet somehow I understand everything they say. In the summer of 2019, while in Mexico, I actually translated a sermon to some of my team because we were too far away from our translator. I just told God to use me so that the rest of our team knew what was being preached, mind you I do not know how to speak Spanish but Holy Spirit is always the best translator. After the sermon, our whole team got back together and everybody verified I had translated correctly.

"ABSOLUTELY NOT!"

As for the more practiced tongues, some say this is the gibber ish-like talk, I was certainly educated against it. But on May 28, 2015, I was driving home from Houston and I heard in my heart God wanted me to pray in tongues. I fought against the urge to speak until it left. Every day I drive 35 minutes from my home to the church and God will tell me He wants me to pray for certain people or situations, but a few days after coming home from Houston, on my way to work, God told me, "I want you to pray for every person that goes to UBC when you get there today..." to which I was excited and replied, "ok!" And then God finished His sentence, "... in tongues." I yelled in my car, "Absolutely not!!!" So I got to the church and prayed like I always did. The next day, God did the same thing, to which I reacted the same way. This happened every day for 10 months. I was beginning to think I was going crazy and that I didn't know God's voice, but I knew it was His voice because it was the same one that would speak to me about healing. After 8 months of repeatedly being told by God to do something I knew I couldn't do, nor did I think was a good thing, I decided I needed more teaching. This was something no Baptist pastor could help me with because I knew what they knew. I needed another perspective, so I began to call other churches in town and schedule appointments and meetings with their pastors. This took me back to my wife's old church, the one I had previously avoided. I eventually talked with pastors from every denomination in town I could find.

NEEDING ANSWERS, AND MAYBE AN ARGUMENT

I learned a lot from the other pastors I spoke with. All of them had unique doctrines and understandings. None completely matched up with the way I had been taught to interpret scripture. It was now mid-March. I called up Ed, the pastor of my wife's original church, again, but this time I had a request. You see, I knew what I had to do. I have always been a fighter. No one could beat me in a debate; no one could out argue me. I was relentless. If I could not out argue you, I would beat you into submission over time. I would not stop until you quit and conceded. I called Ed and said, "Pastor, I need more answers, but this time, I want you to know I am coming to fight. Is that ok?" He agreed with me, and cleared his calendar for 2 days later. I really did need to argue this out of me. We have to be led by the spirit, not the flesh, and not the soul. Our mind is in the soul. If I am led by my thoughts and actions, then I am not being led by the spirit. I understood when it came to tongues, I was operating in my mind, and I need to separate my soul from my spirit, which is what the Word does (Hebrews 4:12). So I went to his office and told him, "I'm going to yell and scream and argue and complain. I need you to stay calm, gentle, and assertive." So we began. He would read a scripture that proved tongues was real, and I would use the same scripture to argue my perspective. We did that for four hours – it was really hard. I did yell, and stand up and shake my bible at him, among other things; meanwhile, he was so gentle and calm. Eventually, I got it all out of my system. Neither one of us was budging, but at least I understood his beliefs.

"SPEAK"

The next night, April 1, 2016, we had our Indian Fellowship, which lasted until about midnight. After it was over, I got in my car and began to drive home. I was about two minutes down the road when I heard God say, "Speak." This meant to speak in tongues. I lost it. I yelled and screamed, "I don't know what you want me to do! I don't know how! I don't even believe it is a good thing! You know what I believe! You know me, God! I can't do this anymore..." He waited for me to finish, and then said, "Speak." I finally quit fighting, "Show me how. Whatever you want, I will do it. I just don't know how." God taught me everything I now believe about tongues in the car that night. I was amazed at what He told me, though. He explained to me how tongues are important for our growth because it forces us to operate in the spirit. When we speak in tongues, we have no idea what is being said. Paul wrote that our mind is unfruitful, but that our spirit is fruitful. Speaking in tongues is also a great beginning to removing the fear of man. So often, I find people who want change privately, but then act completely different around their peers. God explained that He uses tongues to help us get free from fear. The lesson He gave me was only about 5-7 minutes' worth of information. As I have already stated, sometimes God speaks in short, simple sentences that take me a very long time to decipher and understand. Often, God will say a short sentence to me, and it takes me a long time to explain it to someone else. But, with the information He gave me, I was ready to follow His lead. I told God, "I need you to write it out for me, and I will read it." Suddenly, I saw letters written in yellow lights, like the blinking road worker lights you see in construction zones. It was a five-syllable word. I read it in a whisper, and as I did my mouth continued to flow in gibberish. After about 20 seconds of speaking, I was bawling and I forced myself to stop. It was midnight, and I was driving into a small town known as a speed trap, on top of that I was the only car on the road, and there were three police cars. All three pulled out and followed me through town. The lone traffic light turned red, so I stopped as all three cars surrounded me. I was crying so hard there were snot-bubbles. I looked at one police officer, and he just smiled and nodded. The light finally turned green so I started driving again, and all three cars turned around. Immediately, the yellow flashing lights scrolled across my line of sight again. I read the five-syllable word a second time and my mouth went uncontrollably fast. I was so overwhelmed. I stopped about 30 seconds later to try to process everything. At this point I had only been whispering, so I decided I was ready to yell. I told God to do it one more time so that I could yell in tongues, and He immediately sent the word. I yelled for the next 15 minutes, all the way home, in tears. As I pulled into my driveway, it stopped, slowly, fading into whispers and then into nothing.

I use tongues sparingly, now, only when prompted by God. I know a lot of people teach to pray in tongues for hours upon hours, but I have gotten so much from just having conversations with God in English. He reveals a lot to me in my secret place, and I spend hours there. I speak in tongues maybe 2 to 3 minutes per day. For a long time I used tongues when praying for healing. The first time I prayed in tongues for healing was for one of our Indian students. She had a bad crick in her neck. She asked me to pray for it, and I did...6 times without any results. It was still a 10 pain level. I tried yelling, talking, commanding, begging, binding spirits, and interceding for her healing with no change. Then God said, "Pray in tongues." I didn't even know it was something I could do. So I warned her that I was about to pray in tongues, and she said ok, bowed her head and closed her eyes. I might have said four syllables before

I felt like I got hit in the chest and woke up on the other side of the room. Apparently, Holy Spirit pushed me out of the way and I slid about 15 feet across our fellowship hall. When I got up, she was still in the same position that I had started praying. I quickly got up and ran to her, asking how she felt. She thought I was still there, touching her neck, but I wasn't. When she opened her eyes, she was shocked to find me standing in front of her because she was absolutely convinced I was behind her with my hands on her shoulders. I told her to move her neck to see how it was, and as she did her eyes got really wide and said, "Wow! It's completely better!" Honestly, speaking in tongues is still a newer concept which I am still growing in with the direction from Holy Spirit. Even to this day, I have not found anyone else who believes entirely what I do.

LIGHTNINGS FROM HEAVEN

A few months after I began to speak in tongues, I was invited to preach at several churches. One church was holding a youth rally, and had a few different people come speak. They asked me to go last, so I agreed. The person I was following was sort of tough to follow so two of the pastors asked me if they could pray for me. When the second one started praying, I began to feel a tingle on my hands. Then he said something about fire from heaven, and before I knew it I was on the ground screaming in pain from this incredibly intense heat that was all over my entire body. Both pastors were in shock, looking down at me as I screamed and twisted. The one who had been praying squatted down to make sure I was ok, and I grabbed his arm. When I did, he immediately stood straight up and began yelling in tongues. The other one stood there observing, and before he could do anything, I grabbed his arm and he did the same thing. Suddenly the fire and pain left me, so I got up to try to go speak, but my body was still twisting and shaking as if I was being electrocuted.

As I walked to the front of the church, every person I passed either erupted in tongues, or fell down in their pew. It was incredible. As soon as I grabbed the microphone, everything stopped and I preached as if nothing had happened. That started a period of 8 weeks where every Thursday around 1-2 p.m. I would hear something like, "Hey, look up" or "Heads up" about 5 seconds before I would physically see a bolt of lightning come through my office ceiling, hit me in the head and electrocute me for anywhere from 30 seconds to 30 minutes. After the second week, I quit looking up. It was always painful, and very intense. On the eighth week, my wife and I flew with some others to San Diego to attend a conference. On that Saturday, I began asking some of the leadership of the conference if they had any understanding about what I was experiencing. I started by asking one of the leaders. They hadn't heard of this "lightning bolt" encounter, so they left to get another leader. That leader went and got someone else, and this continued until there were at least 18 people there asking me questions. Suddenly, as I was trying my best to describe it to the most recent person to arrive, I heard, "I'm going to show them." I actually stated in fear, "Oh no, He's gonna show you!" before being hit and falling to the ground, with a full dose of these "lightnings." The crowd around me pulled out their phones and started recording it, saying things like, "Wow, the glory is all over Him!" After it stopped, they helped me up and asked me a ton of questions. This group of leaders was the first to have at least some idea of what was happening to me, and their ministry strongly encourages tongues. I have since met and heard of a handful of people having encounters like these. They call them "the Lightnings of God." These Lightnings were released because of the prayers in tongues from the pastor before I went up to preach. The power of praying in tongues cannot be downplayed. A brand new encounter with the Lord opened up to me and many others, many who were innocent bystanders, because of tongues.

ATTACK WHAT YOU'RE AFRAID OF

I think the biggest problem we have with tongues is fear. We fear what we don't know. It is so far outside our mind we find it to be scary, plus it convicts us of our spiritual maturity. Before I awoke, I would sometimes be around people who would speak or pray in tongues. There was always an unfamiliar feeling that would enter the room, and I would always interpret that as a bad thing. It would make me sad or mad, but I now recognize that it was fear that I felt. Where does fear come from? Did God give us a spirit of fear? Two verses in the bible, 2 Timothy 1:7, Romans 8:15 both tell us God does not give us fear, but rather something to counter the fear: The spirit of sonship, the spirit of power, love and a sound mind. Every time I mention tongues at church, I feel fear. Fear isn't from God. God gives love, and love casts out fear. One of my practice for attacking fear is every time I feel fear, I recognize it as a scheme of the enemy and I let love drive it out and conquer it. It's never easy to just push through fear, but I know fear is not a tool of God. Some people teach fear is good because it lets you know you're alive but I believe love is a better indicator you're alive. I want love. I want to love. When I get afraid and don't want to do something, I know I must do it. I focus on God's love, on loving the person the way that God loves them, and I attack the thing I am afraid of. It's amazing how much freedom there is when you let love conquer fear.

When it comes to spiritual battles, tongues are a huge benefit. I have been a part of a number of deliverances in the past few years. There have been times when family members request no tongues be spoken. I never want to give the devil a foothold, and fear is a really big foothold, so if someone is uncomfortable with tongues, I won't use it. However, my first thought is "well, it will take longer." I have learned tongues is very helpful when dealing with multiple demons. Praying in tongues seems to break the person free so much easier than my own words can. Now, there may be a few who think this is an argument that tongues is demonic because the demons understand it. I used to be that guy. Then I read Matthew 12, where the Pharisees said that Jesus casted out demons by using the demonic. That is where Jesus famously said, "*A house divided against itself cannot stand. If Satan drives out Satan, he is divided against himself...*" before proving to them that deliverance is a sign that the Kingdom of God has come. I also love the passage in Matthew 10, when Jesus sent out the twelve, he told them to, "Preach: *the Kingdom of Heaven is near. Heal the sick, raise the dead, cleanse those with leprosy, drive out demons.*" Here in Matthew 12, He says that those acts prove the Kingdom has come. If tongues is effective in defeating the enemy, then it cannot be from the enemy. If it is from the enemy, then Jesus was the enemy, and we know that is not true. We must not allow the enemy to control us with fear. I believe we must be like Paul was: I will become a fool if I must in order to save one soul from the fire. If my family thinks I have lost my mind because I speak in tongues, then so be it. There are hurting people out there that need God's love. If God tells me to use tongues, I will. When He tells me to speak, I do.

THIS IS FOOLISH

I don't want to teach you doctrine. I don't want to convince you of my beliefs. But I will say this about tongues: It is a very odd thing. I often find my mind trying to think when I am speaking in tongues. My mind has nothing else to do, so it tries to direct. It judges my own speech while I am talking. My mind makes fun of me as I make utterances. It is a fascinating experience. It's like Paul wrote in 1 Corinthians 14:14, *"For if I pray, my spirit prays, but my mind is unfruitful."* I only speak in tongues in worship, in my own prayer time (my secret place), or when prompted by God for what I call breakthrough. Breakthrough, for me, is when I am contending for something until I get the desired result. That is breakthrough, whether it is a healing or deliverance, or even wisdom for a dream interpretation or a scripture interpretation. If I am actively praying for someone in person, I will use tongues only after getting approval from them, and even then only when God prompts me to. Of course, if it is just me, I don't need to get permission, but I only do it when prompted. The reason I do not use tongues unless permitted from the other person is because of 1 Corinthians 14. I want to edify. I don't want to cause anyone to stumble.

On that midnight drive home when God taught me about tongues, He shared something else with me. At one point while God was teaching, I interrupted Him with the statement, "God, this is foolish! You want my mind to be unfruitful? That is so different from anything I have ever heard before. It's just so foolish!" Immediately, He reminded me of 1 Corinthians 1:27, where it says, *"God uses the foolish things of the world to confound the wise..."*

INTERPRETING TONGUES

We have a policy at our church about tongues based off the 1 Corinthians chapter 14 passage. If we are singing or praying, and you begin to speak or sing in tongues, it doesn't require interpretation because you are edifying yourself. Your spirit is simply speaking to God. However, if we were not in worship but rather collecting the offering, I am preaching, or we are giving testimonies, and someone starts to speak in tongues, we stop what we are doing and we wait for an interpretation. We expect someone to give the interpretation, because the bible says that tongues accompanied by an interpretation is the highest and greatest of the ways Holy Spirit manifests (1 Cor 14:27-28). Paul writes that prophecy is the highest form of the gifts, unless a tongue is followed with an interpretation. Also, most churches that I know teach about the gifts say that the person who speaks in tongues cannot be the person that interprets the tongue. I don't believe this is true, and I want to show you why. 1 Corinthians 14:13 says, *"For this reason anyone who speaks in a tongue should pray that he may interpret what he says."* Anyone can pray and interpret what is said in our church. I personally want to interpret my own speech. I interpret my own every time I speak in tongues and someone hears me, especially if the person doesn't speak in tongues. I want to be clear about our church, many do not speak in tongues. If I had to estimate I would say maybe 50% do, which makes it important we stay biblically sound so we do not alienate and give reason for the other half of the church to criticize and be closed off to this beautiful gift from Holy Spirit. This whole scenario where someone speaks out loud in tongues rarely happens. Most people only speak in tongues when worshipping or praying, but we have the policy set for if and when it does occur.

SALVATION DOES NOT DEPEND ON IT

Another problem people often have with tongues is the idea that your salvation depends on you speaking in tongues. My mom was severely damaged by this doctrine as a child. She was young, maybe 5 years old when she went to church with her cousins (she was not raised in church). Some people there grabbed her and yelled at her in an attempt to encourage her to speak in tongues. She has mentioned a few times to me just how frightening it was. Here we are, some 60 years later, and she still sometimes cries when the topic of tongues comes up. A few years ago, my wife took my mom to a conference. The people there thought they discerned that my mom was not Holy Spirit filled, and so they began to grab her and plead with her to "give in to Holy Spirit!" The only thing she said she felt was terror and oppression. She said it made her question her faith, and it made her feel incredibly dirty. That is not love.

My mom and I sat in a Subway restaurant one afternoon, just the two of us, and I held her hand as tears fell down her cheeks wishing I could take it all away from her. I apologized to her on their behalf, asked her for forgiveness, and told her why they did what they did. I get it. I want everyone to speak in tongues. It is so amazing, so freeing, so transforming. Just as God taught me that first night before I began to see the word in yellow lights flash across my eyes, "Tongues is designed to get you out of your soul and into your spirit. It is impossible for you to totally surrender to me, and yet still hold back when it comes to tongues. Either surrender it all, or don't." So I held my mom's hand and asked her if I could show her how the Bible teaches us to pray for people to receive tongues. She let me, and I prayed. She didn't speak at that moment, but a peace came and filled her to where she was no longer crying. We need to make sure that love is our motivation in everything we do.

CONQUERING FEAR

Today, when I read Paul's writing on tongues, I am fascinated. *"I would like every one of you to speak in tongues..."* (1

Corinthians 14:5a NIV). I feel the same way. I want you to speak in tongues so bad, but not because it is cool or fun or anything of the sort. I want you to speak in tongues because it will help you grow in the Lord. Hebrews 5 & 6 shows us that tongues is a sign of the mature, a type of solid food for those who through constant use have trained themselves to discern good from evil. Most importantly, I want you to speak in tongues because I believe it means you have conquered fear and allowed Holy Spirit to truly lead you. I wish you could see me right now. I am in tears at the thought that even one person would let go of whatever holds you back. I was terrified of tongues. I hated the idea of tongues. I persecuted those who spoke in tongues, and I have dealt with persecution since I began speaking in tongues. Father's Day 2016 was a hard day for me. My dad was in the church that day. I preached, as usual, but I mentioned that I speak in tongues. We were scheduled to baptize eight people that evening, and somehow tongues came up. After the service, my dad pulled me into my office and yelled at me for what I said. He disowned me right there, on Father's Day. He came back about 2 months later, and we have a great relationship today, but that day was heart breaking. Some of my family continues to talk about me. They even attack my dad, who doesn't speak in tongues, but simply supports me. It seems to me tongues is the most divisive topic in the Church today. I want you to know that God loves you, and I have never experienced anything but miracles and blessings from tongues. I hope sharing scripture as well as sharing my struggles not only educates, but brings a new perspective that encourages you to explore more of God and His Kingdom.

Chapter 5

The Prophetic

The next thing God put on my heart to learn was prophecy, which I found to be very difficult because of my doctrinal background. I had believed we all are given only one gift of the spirit. It's 1 Corinthians 12, *"To one is given..."* When God began to teach me about prophecy, I had another battle inside my head. I was healing, and this passage states that gifts of healing is one of the gifts, and so are tongues and the interpretation of tongues. I realized I was already operating in three gifts. I had to spend time in 1 Corinthians 12-14 because I needed answers. I believed I could only have one gift. How could I be operating in three gifts, and now have God pushing me to develop a fourth gift? That's when I came across verse 6 in chapter 12 and I saw the phrase *"all in all."* If we only start reading in verse 7 and finish the chapter, then we will miss the truth. If we never read chapter 14, we *really* miss the truth. Paul clearly never meant for anyone to think each person only gets one gift of the spirit. Especially when he wrote, *"...but the same God works all workings in all men."* I believe, with that in mind, when we get to verse 7 we see that it is not gifts at all.

God gives the Holy Spirit to all believers and Holy Spirit manifests how He sees fit. Holy Spirit may manifest as a healer, or a word of knowledge, or a prophecy, or tongues depending on the situation. And I believe verse 11 verifies my stance, "*All these are the work of one and the same Spirit, and He gives them to each one, just as He determines.*" First, all of the manifestations (not gifts) come from Holy Spirit. Second, He gives all the manifestations ("them") to each of us. Third, He determines the manifestation according to the time and situation. I believe chapter 14 confirms my belief because he says many are speaking in tongues, and he states in verse 31 everyone in the church can prophesy. So everyone in Corinth could do both, as well as give revelations, instructions, and interpretations (v 26). This seems to be rarely taught yet how amazing is it to know we are not limited to one gift!

One of the problems with believing everyone only gets a single gift from Holy Spirit is it becomes critical to figure out what your gift truly is. I mean, I was afraid of trying out things because I always had the thought, "What if this isn't my gift? What if this is just something I want?" I didn't want to waste time developing my single gift, only to find out it never was mine to begin with. The other side of this is if I did find my gift, then I had absolutely no desire to do anything else. So if my gift was being good money, for example, then I would never need to do any missions because my gift was financing missions. But Jesus gave us all the Great Commission, to GO! The first problem uses fear as a motivation, the second problem creates laziness. Once I surrendered to what God was telling me about all the gifts or manifestations, I had a new-found excitement for studying and evangelizing. It created a deep passion to learn more, and it freed me from the fear and complacency.

WHAT OTHERS DON'T SEE

This was very hard for me to come to terms with, despite the fact I was already operating in three gifts. Religion is very hard to break off sometimes. The old way of thinking doesn't always like the new way of thinking. People who know me many times forget this part. My friends and family do not normally consider my transformation process, they only see the end result, where I smile and love them and encourage them. None of this has been simple or easy. All of it has been amazing, powerful, and joyful, but equally challenging. When you see the results, but don't see the transformational process, you take for granted the struggle. With every step I have taken, it has been difficult to let go of my old way of thinking. I have spent many hours on my knees crying out to my Father. I have yelled at Him, cried to Him, begged Him for relief and help, and I have worshipped Him. He alone knows my journey. He knows how many tears I have cried. He knows the fears I have felt. He knows how my heart breaks for my family, who think I have lost my mind. They pray for me, for God to show me my errors, so that I can be who I used to be. For the life of me, I cannot understand why they want me to go back to what I was: a suicidal, bi-polar, prescription dependent person who ran to men for advice, and never talked to God about anything other than my problems.

What part of that life sounds good? I haven't had a bad day since I woke up and was set free. I have not been angry in years. I am so free, which is exactly what Jesus said I should be. I am not a slave to fear anymore. I know who my Father is. We talk all the time. When I say, "all the time," I want you to know it is ALL the time. Not a second goes by where I am not talking to Him, ever. And I have learned not a second goes by that He is not talking to me. I love who I am, which is a wild sentence for me since the old Jeff hated himself. I honestly love the journey I have been on. I love the transformation. I love the process, as difficult as it has been. I know none of this is God's fault. He never wanted me to think upside-down, but that's exactly how many of us think today. His Kingdom is completely flipped compared to the world we live in. We think belief is important. We think faith and unbelief are opposites. The truth is faith and sight are opposites. Unbelief is not related to faith, in the bible. It's incredible how much of my thinking had to change in order for me to get aligned with God, so that I could hear Him clearly. I have many people come talk to me about how they cannot hear God or have not heard Him in weeks, months, or years. I used to be that person before He woke me up. Now, I hear from Him every second of every day. He speaks infinitely, in infinite ways.

ONLY PROPHETS PROPHESY...OR SO I THOUGHT

One way God speaks to us in through prophecy. I had a difficult time learning about prophecy. Two of the problems I had with prophecy were because of my teachings growing up. The main problem I had was I thought only a Prophet could prophesy. I had no clue everyone can prophesy (Like Paul wrote about the Corinthian church). I did not believe Prophets existed anymore, and since I thought only a Prophet can prophesy, I assumed prophecy had ceased, too. Second, I have never wanted to be a Prophet; I already knew I was a Pastor by calling, so the office of a Prophet was not on the table for me. My ignorance on the topic of callings, offices, and giftings caused me to blend an office of a Prophet with prophecy so I had a hard time letting go of fear of stepping into another calling. The first time I learned about prophecy I was encouraged to attempt a form of prophecy, and I was terrified. It was actually about two months after I woke up from my spiritual coma. I learned from Bob Hazlett prophecy is not just about telling the future. Prophesying is hearing intimate things about a person from God, and telling them what you hear. Words of knowledge are when you know things about someone you've never met, and words of wisdom are when you have an answer for someone who has been asking God something or when you have advice about something that pertains to a prayer. Both of these Words (mentioned in 1 Corinthians 12) happen often, when I have conversations with people. Over the years, it has increasingly become more common to experience these Words.

These days, God even gives me Words of knowledge and wisdom for others while I am in my secret place with Him. On December 26, I was in prayer and suddenly had a thought of a young man, who formerly attended our church, was going to move to Kingsville after graduating 4 years prior. I had not seen him in quite some time, and I would not think about him on my own. Interestingly, while I was praying, I even heard the day he would move. Then, about a month later, I was given another Word about his future roommate moving back to Kingsville after being gone for almost 3 years. Three months later on the exact day, they moved into an apartment together.

If it has to do with the future, that is prophesying. If it has to do with your past and present, the bible calls it a word or message of knowledge, depending on your translation. I call it a word of knowledge. Words of knowledge are fun, now, but they were hard for me at first, since I didn't know God's voice very well.

"YOU'RE A BUFFALO"

My first attempt at prophecy was in Houston, with Bob. He told us to go around and find someone who we didn't know and stand next to them. I did. I found a man about 6'4" and 230 pounds. He was a big guy. As soon as I saw him I thought about a buffalo. Then, once we were paired up, Bob told us to pray and ask God to show us an animal that embodied the person we were with. Well, I was focused on buffalo. Then Bob told us to tell the person what animal we heard/saw, and why they are that animal. I went first. I told him he was a buffalo, of course, but I didn't have a reason. I started asking him questions and making statements. Everything I said was way wrong. I told him buffalos move in giant herds, but he told me he prefers to work alone. I proceeded to explain in the Native American culture they use every part of the buffalo for their family and for the community, he tells me he has no family. I talked about the thickness of the buffalo's hide and him having tough skin and he responded with "no, that's not me at all". It was so embarrassing, every thought I had landed nowhere with him. Then, it was Buffalo's turn to tell me. He said, "You're a turtle because you are very slow moving. You take a long time to process things. You don't like to change directions, and when it comes to spiritually moving, it is very difficult for you. However, once you get turned around, nothing stops you from moving in that direction. You are very determined, and no outside interference distracts you. Your shell is strong and healthy, God loves this about you. He enjoys your steadfastness, and He is proud that you recently turned around." I was floored. I called this guy a buffalo, got nothing right about him, and he knew me better than I knew myself. He had a word of knowledge about me, and then proceeded to prophesy. It was incredible. I had a lot to learn.

SYMPATHY PAINS

For the next year, I was determined to figure out words of knowledge. I would sit in a chair by the doors outside Hobby Lobby and ask people for prayer, attempting to give words of knowledge. It took a while for me to develop hearing accurately in that first year. In that time period, if I did not pray for healing, I could not get a word of knowledge either. About 8 months in, however, I realized the subtle impressions and feelings I was getting while praying for healing, were words of knowledge all along. I would suddenly feel pain as I walked past someone, or for example, I would be sitting in a restaurant, and a waiter would come up to me. As soon as they got close to me, I would feel a sharp pain in my left ankle. Now I had complete reconstruction done on my right ankle in 2004, but my left ankle is strong. If it hurts, I know that is odd. So I figured to ask the waiter how their left ankle was and sure enough the response "how did you know?" followed by God healing through prayer because He highlighted the pain and wanted it removed. Sometimes, it will be my back or my shoulder. I have learned to identify "sympathy pains" as something another person is dealing with, but I feel it so that I can pray for it. Sympathy pains can be a type of word of knowledge.

My church runs a Healing Rooms ministry every Thursday night. One night, a woman came in for prayer over her left knee. Our standard procedure for Healing Rooms is having a team of three people in a room to pray for a single person for 15 minutes. One of the male team members went into the waiting room and escorted the woman into the prayer room.   As they walked into the room together, I suddenly felt my old back pain flare up really bad. I asked the woman how her back was, and she said she was fine. I was about to ask her if she was sure, when I suddenly knew it was the guy who went to get her. I turned to him and said, "It's your back! Your back is hurting!" He looked at me in a little bit of shock and confirmed it. So we prayed for her, and then we prayed for him, both were healed. Our team member was there to pray for others and it never dawned on him that he needed prayer until the word of knowledge, what a loving God we serve.

A CHRISTIAN WALKS INTO A BANK...

A fun story about a word of knowledge happened in June 2019 goes like this: It was a Friday morning and I had to go to the bank. As I got out of my car to go inside (I love to go inside and talk to people now. I used to go to the bank after midnight and put my check in through the ATM machine so I didn't have to deal with anyone) I began to feel a terrible pain in my left knee. Now, I had a reconstructive knee surgery in 1999 on my left knee so sometimes it does hurt. As I walked across the parking lot, I felt this dull pain begin to reside inside. As I got closer to the building, it increased in pain. When I got inside I could barely put any weight on my leg. I could actually feel my meniscus hurt like it did when I tore it in '99, and I also felt this agonizing throbbing, grinding, dull pain all over. I thought to myself, "I guess it's about to rain." I got in line, deposited my check and had a pleasant conversation with the teller. Then I started to walk outside. I passed one of the employees as I exited the building, and I saw pain in her eyes. Still, I thought this was my pain. I was telling myself that when I got home, I would pray for healing. I took two steps outside and my knee completely gave out. I was on the sidewalk, on my hands and my knees and in tremendous pain. Then, I forced myself up on my feet to get to my car, on the opposite side of the parking lot, and took my first step. The pain was completely gone! Immediately, I knew I was experiencing a word of knowledge through a sympathy pain. I turned around and walked inside the Bank, which was empty except for the seven female employees inside. I was so focused on the mission that I didn't think about how my actions would come across. I held up my hands and yelled out, "Excuse me, can I have your attention!" They all froze and looked up at me in terror, thinking I was attempting to rob the bank. I dropped my hands and said, "Oh no! I'm just a Christian and I believe God told me to come back inside to pray for someone..." I went on to explain to them about the knee pain and that I believed God wanted to heal whoever it was. Then I asked, "So does anyone in here have pain in your left knee?" Two women raised their hands, the lady I passed as I left, and the teller who had helped me. I asked the teller what was wrong with her knee, and she stated it was a torn meniscus. Then the other woman stated she had arthritis in her left knee. It was exactly what I had been feeling. I prayed with them and both were completely healed right there. Then two other women came running and asked me to pray for their shoulder and back. So we prayed and all four were completely healed with one prayer.

MORE WORDS OF KNOWLEDGE

Another word of knowledge would be dreams or visions. I get those, as well, now. I will be talking to someone and suddenly see a vision. When I describe it to them, they usually say something along the lines of, "That was my dream last night!" It doesn't happen often, I have probably experienced that 10 times in 4 years, but it has happened. My basic definition of a word of knowledge is anything that proves God knows someone. It could be physical pain, it could be a dream they have had (like Daniel did with King Nebuchadnezzar), or it could be something else. One example I can talk about happened when

Robby Dawkins came to our church in 2017. We had a time of ministry with an altar call, and many people came forward. One young lady was standing there alone. I approached her and suddenly had a mental image of these yellow flowers. I described them to her, how I could see them falling down onto something, and then I said, "He is with God." I didn't have any idea what that meant or why I had even said it. It just came out of my mouth before I could explain it. The young lady fell to her knees and began to cry uncontrollably. I let her cry and began to minister to others, but as soon as I was able to I returned to ask her what it meant. She informed me the flowers I described were her grandfather's favorite flower, and that she had just buried him, and she had put some of those flowers on his casket. She had no idea if he was a Christian or not, but when I said what I did she instantly knew he was in Heaven. This is why words of knowledge are part of the prophetic area. They are messages from God, showing people that He knows them, loves them, and is seeking more of a relationship with them.

WORDS OF WISDOM

The next part of the prophetic I discovered was words of wisdom, which I am still learning about. To me, words of wisdom are answers to your questions you ask the Lord in prayer. God speaks to us in many ways: dreams, visions, and prayer are some of the ways. But questions come up because of these conversations with God sometimes. It is common for people to receive a dream from God, but not know how to interpret the dream. This is one way that a message of wisdom would come. If you ask me to interpret your dream, I have two choices: One, I can do my best to tell you what I think. Two, I can ask God to show me what He was telling you. The second one would be a word of wisdom.

"ROAD WORK ENDS HERE"

I was talking to someone a while ago, and suddenly I interrupted her because I knew she had been in prayer about something.

"You've been praying to God about what job you should take"

She was shocked, "How could you know this? I haven't told anyone."

"Because you have been talking to God about it for some time and He is telling me you missed His answer. He wants you to know though He will tell you first thing in the morning. You are wondering if you should stay at work here, or move up north."

"Jeff, I don't understand how, but you are so right! I will be waiting in the morning."

"Yes, but it won't be an answer with words. It will be a road sign. The first you see tomorrow morning." The next day, I got a text of a picture of a road sign: "Road work ends here." She immediately knew she was supposed to stay and work in her hometown and not travel north. I really enjoy words of wisdom.

WORD OF WISDOM *AND* KNOWLEDGE

There is nothing like hearing God answer your questions. God speaks to us one way or another. Sometimes, He speaks through us. A few months ago, I was in San Antonio visiting friends, and we went to lunch. As we were leaving the restaurant, I felt the need to leave $20 at the register for the next family who couldn't pay. I gave instructions to the cashier, as one of my friends, Rajitha, prayed for the owner. The rest of us waited at the door while she prayed. As we left to walk to our cars, a woman with 4 kids followed us out of the place. She then said meekly, "Excuse me sir, but thank you so much. That was so kind of you." I was caught off guard at first, but then I realized the $20 was used for her. I smiled and told her it was my pleasure. Then she spoke again, "Sir, I heard you are a pastor. Would you please pray for me?" I smiled, and we all stopped to talk with her. We walked her and her children to her car, and then started praying. While praying, I heard God say she was currently in an abusive relationship (this is a word of knowledge). So I looked at her, and told her to look in my eyes. When she did, I told her, "The relationship you are in is not what God wants for you. Love never does what has happened to you. Take your kids and move back home." (This is a word of wisdom) She started bawling. I did not want to say, "Your boyfriend is beating you," because I did not want anyone else to hear that. My friends each prayed for her, and she got in her car. As we walked back to our cars, my two friends both said, "You know, her boyfriend is beating her." We all heard the same thing. Holy Spirit revealed a word of knowledge and a word of wisdom to protect but also reconcile this precious woman and her children to the Father.

THE PILLAR

The office of a Prophet is definitely a new revelation for me. I was taught the Prophets were an Old Testament office, that they no longer exist because the Bible was finished and there is no need for Prophets anymore. My denominational upbringing suppressed the truth, which prevented me from being exposed to the office of Prophet, entirely. In 2017, I met a Prophet for the first time, and immediately I felt something like blinders were removed from my eyes. I became spiritually hungry and passionate to see more. As I have progressed, I have learned the difference between a Prophet and prophecy. Even still, prophesying is something I am in the process of learning. I tend to want to stay very general and non-specific when giving a prophecy because I don't want to get it wrong. The idea of telling someone their future is scary. But I have met some prophets, and it is absolutely undeniable it's the office they carry. Dennis Goldsworthy-Davis and Danny Aguilar are two prophets God has connected me with, both from Great Grace International Church in San Antonio, Texas. You know it as soon as they speak. They have the office of Prophets, and it's impossible to deny because the experience is like sitting down with Isaiah. You just *know*. My friend Danny prophesied on October 14, 2017 that "men of fire would come to the church with questions, soon." That sounded fun to me. I was excited to see Christians on fire for Jesus come to our church to learn more about God.

Two months later, on December 13, 2017, I was driving to church when God told me, "Today, I want to worship WITH you." Every day, God gives me instructions for the day. He tells me what He wants me to do. It could be prayer, singing, playing drums, reading scripture, calling 50 people, or anything else. I had never heard God say He wanted to worship *with* me. I didn't quite understand the twist, but I was excited to learn! So I told myself that I was just going to lock my office door and worship with God all day. As I drove up to the church, there were 5 people standing outside my office, waiting for me. That hasn't happened since. Well, I opened my office, and started talking to each one. People come to my office daily, but never have I had five people standing outside my door before I got there. That day, it was constant. For 9 hours, I had someone in my office. From 8:00

a.m. until 5:14 p.m., there was at least one person sitting in my office. At 5:14 p.m., the last person left. I looked outside and saw no one else, so I locked the door, turned off the lights, and started to worship. It was 5:15 by the time I finally got on my knees. As soon as I started to worship, I knew it was different. I still don't know what exactly it was I felt, but there was a presence in the room I have not experienced any other moment of my life. Then, at 5:21 p.m., someone knocked on my door. I worshipped for literally 6 minutes. I turned on the lights, unlocked the door and let him in. We talked until 5:44 p.m.

As he left, I contemplated worshipping again, but our services start at 6:00 p.m. and I hadn't had any time to prepare. So I got to work, quickly. I went into the fellowship hall, where we have our Wednesday night service, and laid out all the papers. Larry and Sabra, our faithful church couple, came in first. It was about 5:55 p.m. at this time. To make mention, it was December 13, so we had Christmas decorations up. We have a tree by a window in the room, and it has gold lighting. When I looked at it, I saw a blinking red glow on the tree. I walked around the tree to see where the red was coming from, and when I looked out the window, I saw emergency lights flashing. I told Larry, "I think the police are here."

I walked over to the door, but before I could grab it, it swung open, and there in the doorway was a fireman in full gear! He shouted, "Where is the fire?"

Larry looked at me in shock, and I looked back at him in bewilderment. I spoke up, "Sir, I have been here all day, and I am not aware that there has been a fire."

"Well, someone called us that there was a fire here."

"Ok sir, come with me, we will look in every room." We thoroughly inspected every single room.

The sanctuary was the last room we got to, and when we

opened it up, the fireman said in frustration, "There hasn't been a fire here. I don't know what he was thinking."

I talked with the fireman a little about whether or not I needed to fill out paperwork and the things that needed to be done as we walked out to the front parking lot. It was then I realized the scene that was set up. Three fire trucks and 12 men in full gear, masks, some had axes, all standing around waiting for instructions.

I was walking the firefighter to the trucks when a pickup truck whipped into the parking lot between two of the fire trucks. The man driving the truck grabbed a hat and a coat as he jumped out yelling, "What are y'all doing standing around? Get to work!"

The fireman I had been with interrupted, "Sir, I inspected this whole place, there is no fire."

This just made the chief, the man from the pickup truck, more determined, "Son, don't tell me there wasn't a fire! I saw it myself! Heck, I called it in! It was coming out of that room right there!" He pointed as he said that, and he pointed at my office.

I couldn't hold it in. I stepped in, "That's my office, sir. I have been in there all day. I guarantee you there was no fire in that room."

He turned to me and said, "Young man, I came out of City Hall at 5:15 p.m., and I saw a pillar of smoke stretching up to the heavens. I was with the mayor. I ran to my truck, and followed the trail back to that door, where smoke was pouring out. I'm telling you, son, 45-odd minutes ago I saw a pillar of smoke going all the way straight up into the heavens. I called this in. There is no mistake here."

It was at that moment I heard God say, "I told you I was going to worship WITH you today." I tried to explain the story to the chief, but he didn't understand.

His response to my story was, "Maybe I got the wrong

place. Let's drive around until we find what's left of the building." As they drove away, I called some of my friends to tell them. When I told Danny, he asked, "Hey, didn't I prophesy that men of fire would come with questions?" I was floored! He did. Prophecy is amazing. In the last several years, our church has seen many prophecies come to pass.

PROPHECY STILL PROMINENT...

I know there are people out there, denominations even, that teach John the Baptist was the last prophet, and there are no prophets any more. I was raised that way. It's one of the reasons prophecy was so hard for me at first. John the Baptist was the last of the Old Testament prophets. If he is the last prophet, then what is Agabus? He first appears in Acts 11:27, as a prophet from Jerusalem, who operated under the Spirit of God. So obviously there are New Testament prophets who appear after John died. So John cannot be the last prophet. Also, as I have previously written, Paul wrote that all of Corinth could prophesy. It is important that we never make a doctrine because of what we do not see, when scriptures say something entirely different. It's actually what Jesus preached about when he said, "You have heard it said... but I say..." We need to really follow the Word of God.

...BUT BE AWARE

I am aware not all prophecies are accurate. About a year ago, a group of our college aged students went to a church in Corpus Christi because they were hosting a worship service. After the service, the pastor invited his team to begin prophesying to people. One of the ladies in the ministry team approached my group and began to tell them only of their past sins and failures.

She told them things that were not true. Because our students were trying to be humble, some of them actually received it as a word from God. A few days later, they came to me very oppressed and confused about what had been said. It took me a few days to help them get free again.

There needs to be a distinction between prophecy of the Old Testament and of the New Testament. The Bible says John the Baptist was the last of the Old Testament prophets. When I read about the prophets of the Old Testament, I notice they bring up sins and speak about judgement. There are many examples of this as found in the books of Jeremiah, Isaiah, Ezekiel or even in the life of Samuel. The prophets were the voice of God to the people, and they hadn't had their sins paid for, so when someone like David sinned, it required a prophet like Nathan to tell him that his sinned required the death of his son. Sometimes, people are not taught about this, and so when they receive a word from Holy Spirit, they give it to the person without the right perspective. In the New Testament, Paul wrote that *God has hidden gold inside of our jars of clay* (2 Corinthians 4:7). As people who live in this New Testament era, we are supposed to prophesy to the gold we see inside of people, not the dirt.

"GO BACK TO YOUR FATHER"

One day, at our Healing Rooms, a young woman came in for prayer. She didn't need healing, but just wanted someone to pray for her. I was up first in our group of three people to pray, and as soon as I started, I saw a very tough scene in my mind. I saw her with a man at least twice her age, and that she had dropped out of school to be with him. I also saw they had done some bad things, and that she had turned her back on God. I knew not to tell her any of this, because she already knew what

she had done. I finished my prayer, and then stepped away in
order to get more direction from God. Meanwhile, the other
two people prayed for her. I sought the Lord for guidance, and
all I heard was, "Be gentle with her, and tell her to go to her
father." So, after the others prayed, I stood in front of her again.
She had tears running down her face. I asked her to look up
into my eyes, and I began, "I need you to know that God
showed me who you live with and what you have been doing.
He is aware, and He showed me so that I could tell you this: Go
home. Leave him, go back to your father and apologize. And
give your life to Jesus. He loves you. He just wants to have a
relationship with you again."

She was in shock. She confessed everything, and then told
me her father was a pastor of a church in a town about an hour
or two north of our church. She said she knew the word was
from God, and that all she wanted was to be close to Jesus. She
was tired of the life she had chosen, but didn't know how to go
back home. I told her to just go, and to tell her dad everything. I
could have told her how wicked and evil she had been. I could
have told her how dumb it was to drop out of school. I could
have made her feel terrible, but she already felt terrible. Her
conscience was already moving, and Holy Spirit was calling her
home. Why should I try to do what Holy Spirit was so clearly
doing already? I just needed to encourage her, and help her see
that God loved her. I heard somewhere that a prophecy should
be like a kiss from God. It should ignite passion for Him, not
fear or regret. We have to practice discipline when God gives
us a word for someone. I am so glad He has taught me to be
slow to speak, and to lean on His understanding and instructions in times like this.

The prophetic is a fascinating thing to experience. I never
feel confident before speaking. I struggle with confidence in
hearing. It feels like I am standing on the edge of a cliff and if I

speak, it will be like jumping off into a dark void. But it never ends like that. Even when I'm wrong, and I have been wrong a lot, people are kind and encouraging. Some are impressed with the level of faith required to take such a risk. When you are hearing correctly, which has been the majority of my experiences, everyone is blown away. I've heard it said, "Healing is like a hug from God, but prophecy is like a kiss."

Chapter 6

Spiritual Warfare

I started learning about spiritual warfare a long time before my awakening. On my 20th birthday, I had my first encounter with Ebenezer. This is a complicated story, and will take a lot of background information in order to make sense. I was working at a Christian Summer camp in East Texas, at the time. I hardly ever go to sleep before midnight; it's always been that way. When I was a child, my grandfather nicknamed me the White Tornado, because I had white hair and I was so hyperactive that most people couldn't deal with me. A few years later, I was diagnosed with ADHD. Now, I must say ADHD was a real struggle for me at the time. From Kindergarten until 6th grade, I never heard a teacher actually teach a single lesson all the way through. Within five minutes of their first lecture, I was already gone, in my own mind, screaming inside about how I needed to pay attention even though it was impossible.

In 6th grade, I finally gave in to taking medicine. I never wanted to take anything for ADHD, but school was too difficult for me to continue without that little white pill. The first day I took one pill, I heard every teacher speak the entire class. I remember I couldn't wait to get home and tell my mom, a teacher herself, that I had heard my teachers for the first time in my life. It was amazing that my mind would actually let me listen to someone speak. Life became so much easier because of the pills, but even then, ADHD really affected my life. I was so hyperactive that I would go days without sleeping. When I say days, I mean as many as 7 days without a minute of sleep. As soon as lights were turned off, I would wake up and get hyper. Then I would get up and play with toys, or video games, or study football. (Not until I met my wife, did I actually sleep a full night through, and never before midnight). I would act asleep, as a child, so I wouldn't get into trouble until my parents finally fell asleep. But on my 20th birthday at the camp, something different happened. I felt very tired and decided to clock out early and I went to sleep around 7:00 p.m..

It was during my sleep that everything went crazy with Ebenezer. The way he introduced his presence was something my brother James will never forget. He knew I must be sick to be in bed so early, so at some point in the evening or night, he came to check on me (he worked at the same camp). When he opened my bedroom door, I was asleep in the bed. It was at this point he noticed all the paper in the room. Apparently, I had torn up hundreds of sheets of paper and written in red marker all over them. I had stuck them on the walls, I had filled the floor with them, and they were on the bed. Every word that I had written was filth. He saw all this and decided he needed to speak up, "Uh, Jeff? You ok?" He told me my eyes popped open, I smiled, and then my blanket and sheets flew off my bed and hit the opposite wall. As that happened, I quickly and easily stood up in the bed for a moment before levitating above the bed. His girlfriend's dog rushed in, barking. I raised my hand and squeezed the air, and the dog dropped with a squeal.

James rushed into the room and grabbed the dog only moments before I flicked my wrist, sending both the dog and him out of the room and hitting the hallway wall. As he hit the wall, the door slammed shut and locked.

A few hours later, I awoke with the worst sore throat. As I left my room to get some water, I found my brother with our boss and a counselor all standing in the living room. It was about 3:00 a.m. at this point. Those guys never came over to the house, so I tried asking them what they were doing, but my throat was so raw that I could not make a sound. That's when our boss asked me if I was okay. Then the counselor asked me some questions. I had no idea what they were talking about, so I went back to bed. Then I dreamed everything. When I woke up the next morning I assumed it was all a dream, but when I walked into the living room, all three men were still there. I asked my brother about the dream, and he told me it all happened exactly like I described. I asked him why my throat was so sore; his answer was, "You were speaking in the scariest voice, and in weird gibberish nonsense. It was crazy." I went off to work, weed eating and mowing the acres of forest before lifeguarding at the pool. My boss seemed a little scared of me, and he asked me about my salvation more than once.

The next six weeks were really tough. I would flip all of the sudden, going from laughing and having fun to screaming and breaking things because of this wave of anger. I saw things. I heard voices. I would see this demon everywhere. It was a horrible experience. Eventually, it got to a point where I had a fight with the demon in a driveway, while others watched. I got picked up and thrown. That was my last day of work. I drove 8 hours the next day to get to my grandfather's house to ask for help. I knew he would at least be able to direct me to some help. That's where I learned of Ebenezer's name. My grandfather and he had a long conversation, and then my grandfather told him it was time for him to leave. There was a big battle after that. My grandfather won. I was shocked. I had come to believe that the demon was so strong nothing could beat it. My grandparents sent me home to get some rest.

My parents live about 30 minutes from my grandparents' house. I made it about 5 minutes down the road before Ebenezer appeared in my car. I was so scared, but I knew I had family who lived nearby. I drove to my aunt's house, and I asked her to come outside because she had visitors in the house and I didn't want to cause a scene. There in her front yard, I tried to explain to her what had been happening to me, and as I was talking the demon approached from behind her. I was terrified for her, so I began begging her to go back inside for her own safety, but she fought for me, saying, "No! Jeff is a child of God. He belongs to Jesus! You cannot have him!" The demon suddenly vanished. She then put me in my car and drove me back to my grandparents' house while my uncle followed her. I think they also called my parents, because my parents have talked about being there, but I have no recollection, all I remember was the fear inside me. There was another fight, but this one was a lot easier, and the demon left. He kept coming back, for another four months actually. Just about every day, Ebenezer would come to my dorm room, where I would send him back where he came from. I learned from that experience demons are powerful, but they obey authority from Christians.

When I became a youth minister, I had a youth who told me she thought a demon was in her house. So I went and cleansed the house, no big deal. That was basically the extent of my knowledge of spiritual warfare until my awakening. It didn't take long afterward before I noticed some demonic spirit activity when dealing with healing. Sometimes when I would pray for people I would observe that when I prayed, the pain would go from a 10 to a 6 to a 4 and then stay at a 4. Other times it would increase back up to a 6 or even a 10. I would get so puzzled by this. Sometimes, it would go down to a 1 before moving to another part of the body. What may have started in the shoulder would suddenly move to the wrist or ankle. Then it would shift to a knee or to their back. For example, my wife and I went to a conference where Bob Hazlett and Todd White were speaking. We prayed for a man who suffered from fibromyalgia. We prayed for his eyes, then his stomach (which was fascinating because as we prayed for his stomach, he began burping. His stomach had so much gas that he lost 3 inches in his waist) before the pain moved to his neck. Even though we had been praying for his stomach, we now had to pray for his neck, which then became prayers for his knees, then his shoulders. While we were doing this, he lost 45 pounds, right there in front of our eyes! Another person was praying for a lady nearby, and he seemed to be chasing her pain as it moved all over her. The pain would disappear as the man prayed for her, but it would suddenly pop up in a completely different place. I could hear this man basically praying for the same 3 places over and over again, as it would leave and shift to the next location. The man was getting more and more confused. It can be very confusing, trying to battle with a spirit.

Just a few months ago, one of our members went to our Healing Room for prayer. She was in the room, while I was witnessing to a man out in the parking lot. The man was healed of a back problem, and surrendered his life to Jesus. It was awesome. I love it when big, strong men cry because of Jesus' love. As I finished with the man, I saw the woman walking to her car. I ran over to her to see how she was doing. She had fibromyalgia as well, and was having the most trouble in her wrist. She told me, "When they started praying I would say the pain was a 7. Then they got to praying and the pain was absolutely a 10, it was so bad I had to sit down. But they kept praying, so the pain went back down to a 7, and that's where it is now. I told her I wanted to pray. She allowed me, and the pain in her wrist went down to a 0, but now there was a pain in her right shoulder blade. I prayed for that and it moved to her left shoulder blade. I knew this was spiritual warfare. So I spoke straight to the demon. I bound its mouth and commanded it to leave her alone and immediately all the pain left her, because they must obey.

EVERYTHING IN YOUR LIFE IS SPIRITUAL

Spiritual warfare is a complicated topic. There are whole books and lessons dedicated to it. There needs to be more. I don't have the time or space to teach you everything there is to know about spiritual warfare, but I will write some basic principles and scriptures to help you get started. The first thing you need to know is everything in your life is spiritual. Let me say that again with emphasis: EVERYTHING in your life IS SPIRI-TUAL. Hebrews 11:3 states that everything that was made started out in the invisible spiritual world before it became physically visible. So this book you are reading started out spiri-tual, and slowly manifested into the physical over the course of a few years. (This book was prophesied multiple times before I finally gave in to sit down and write it.) The Mona Lisa was first spiritual before it was physical. Music is the same. All of creation follows this same principle. Everything is spiritual. Even a broken ankle is spiritual before it is physical. You name it, if it is physical, it started off spiritual. Is a sickness physical? Then it started off as spiritual. I asked God that question about a year ago. His response to my question was, "Read Hebrews 11:3." I love it when God tells me to read a passage I haven't read or am not familiar with. This caused me to ask Him another question, "So if everything is spiritual, are You the cause of everything?" I already knew the answer based off John 10:10: No, God doesn't cause the broken leg, the loss of a job, cancer, or anything else. I know we want to say He is the reason, but He is not. I asked God for proof. He took me to Ephesians 6:12. God taught me the hierarchy of the enemy and He directed me to a few books.

Allow me to dive into scripture for a second to explain myself; 2 Timothy 1:7 says, *"For God did not give us a spirit of fear, but a spirit of power, of love, and of a sound mind."* What this means is a spirit of fear does not come from God, but comes from someone else. The spirit of fear comes from the enemy. So God gives good spirits, and the enemy gives bad spirits. Hebrews 1:14 tells us angels give good spirits. The bible states that our own tongue has the power of life or death (Proverbs 18:21). I believe this is referring to spiritual things. From my research into the bible and from these books and men I have been blessed to talk to, I have come to believe the hierarchy of Ephesians 6:12 is an incredible source to learn about the warfare we are in. In Ephesians 6:12, there are 4 different entities named by Paul, and the Greek names have much more meaning than our English translations let on. The Greek words are Archa, Exousias, Kosmokratoras, and Pneumatika. Archas are where we get the word "archangels," Exousias means "legal scribes," and Kosmokratoras are actually demons that are worshipped by man in ancient Greece. But Pneumatika is the word for "spirit or breath." This is why I can assuredly say God, angels, and humans can create spirits (we all breathe and speak).

YOU'RE A PETROS

We were born into this war. Even before you were born, you were entangled in a war for your soul. The crazy thing to me is as long as I thought like a man, I lost every time. The enemy was so much more powerful than I was. My mind was set too low. Matthew 16 is a great chapter; I love it because that is where Simon becomes Peter. That's where we get our identity. The name Peter comes from the Greek word petros, which means a throwing stone. What Jesus was saying at Caesarea Philippi was everyone who believes and confesses faith in Jesus will be used as a throwing stone to destroy the devil, just like David used a throwing stone to take out Goliath. I am a petros, a throwing stone. Jesus calls me the weapon that killed Goliath. I love that. I have a throwing stone from Caesarea Philippi I picked up when visiting Israel in 2017 with my wife. I keep that stone on my desk in my office at the church. It is a great reminder of who I am, and what I am supposed to do with my life every day. Getting back to the rest of the story, immediately after the name conversion in Matthew 16, Peter makes a mistake and Jesus calls him Satan. Everyone seems to know the first part of that verse: *"Get behind me Satan!"*, but I hardly ever hear anyone quote the whole thing: *"Get behind me Satan! You are a stumbling block to me, for you do not have in mind the things of God, but the things of men."* Right here, in red and white, you have Jesus saying we cannot think like men. We must think like God. Paul learned the lesson. He wrote about it in 1 Corinthians 2:16 when he finished the chapter with, *"...But we have the mind of Christ."* As long as we think like men, we will stumble and fall. When we think like God, like Jesus, which is perfectly possible, we can rise above the enemy. I used to think demons were so powerful that we can never defeat them, but only hope they will ignore us. I was convinced we could never beat a demon in a battle. That was years ago, before I learned to think with the mind of Christ.

"YES AND AMEN"

A few years ago, we had a family in our church who spoke no English, and did not believe in Jesus. They were from another country, and worked at the university across the street from the church. We have a ministry team that works with the professors and spends a lot of time with them, in hopes of showing them God's love so that they let go of atheism and come to a relationship with Jesus. This family was one of those – they were devout atheists. Over the course of the semester the wife began to get sicker and sicker. Then she started speaking in another voice. She would go days and weeks without eating. What was even worse about the situation is she was pregnant. We tried to help her, recommending doctors for her to see, picking up medications she was prescribed. The help I really wanted to give her was to get rid of this demon, but the husband would not let me near her. This went on for months. Eventually, a few months after she had given birth and continued to digress in both her physical and mental health, the husband gave in and let me stop by one night. She knew no English, and so I brought a translator from our church with me. Like many people, the translator did not believe in demons.

When we arrived at the apartment she was very ill and had not eaten in two weeks, so I sat down on the floor beside her. She immediately started talking to the translator, who was on the opposite side of the room, which means she turned her head away from me. I looked at her very closely, and said gently and quietly, "Be quiet and come out." Immediately, her eyes turned to me, looked right in mine and she said to the translator, "Tell him to stop praying." I smiled and informed them both that I was not talking to God. "I am talking to you, inside her. Be quiet and come out." She then turned her whole head to me and repeated through the translator, "No praying!" I relented for a few seconds. Then I said, "It's time for you to leave this woman and go." At this, the woman turned to me and yelled in a man's voice and in English, "STOP IT NOW!" My translator panicked and began to try to open the door to run away. I calmly yet assertively stated, "Leave her now! You have to go! By the blood of Jesus, I command you to leave!" My translator was already running down the apartment staircase outside, so I had to get up and go. I found out she ate for the next four days, before suddenly stopping again.

Four weeks went by, and then I got a phone call from the husband. He was scared because his wife was coughing up blood now. They had taken her to the hospital, but she refused to cooperate, so they sent her home. I called a pastor friend and asked him to come with me to see her and get the demon out of her. This was my first deliverance, and I wanted some back up, I was very nervous. I prayed for a few hours the morning before I headed over to pick him up. When I got in my car, I told God I needed Him to move in a mighty way. That was when I heard Him say "My Kingdom is not a Kingdom of yes and no", He had already said yes to my prayers and was going to set her free. I felt all my anxiety and worry leave instantly.

I picked up the pastor and we drove to the apartment. Upon parking, I had a vision of the whole place. I had only been in the living room before, but in this vision, I saw where everyone was sitting, and I saw her in a yellow room on a bed. I told the pastor what would happen, where she would be, and what the plan was. As soon as we both walked into the apartment and our feet touched the carpet the man's voice I had heard come out of the woman a month before began yelling, "No! Get them out! Make them leave now!" My pastor friend turned to me and was startled. I told him the plan again, to turn left down to the end of the hall where her bedroom was, to go through the door and turn left, that she was laying there in a yellow bed. He began walking that way, and I made everyone else leave. My translator and her husband were there this time, both a little nervous, but willing to do whatever was necessary to help. I asked them to protect the doors, not to let her out, no matter what.

We both got to the bedroom, and it was a nightmarish scene. We were both filled with compassion because she was so close to death. She weighed less than 70 pounds. Take my word, it was not a good thing to see. We rushed to her, my pastor friend arriving first. He gently reached out to hold her hands with a fatherly affection and started speaking love and comfort over her. I got to the edge of the bed, and suddenly the woman stood up and screamed with that other voice, "No! Not him!" The door was not held shut, and she ran out into the living room. I followed closely behind. When the demon got to the living room, there was nowhere else it could go. It turned in every direction, and then finally toward me. Without another sound, it just left. The woman collapsed to the ground.

We loved on her, holding her hands, speaking life into her. We told her she would be okay. She needed the translators again. She informed us her mother had been a Christian, but she had died. She blamed God for the cancer that took her mother. She confessed her hatred, and then let it go. She knew God had set her free. We then commanded a spirit of strength to enter her so that she could eat. Immediately she got up and walked to the kitchen. She cracked open a watermelon and began eating it. Within a week, her entire family of seven had accepted Christ. They moved away a few months later, but the last I heard was she was doing great.

SPIRITS AND DEMONS: NOT THE SAME THING

I know a lot of people don't believe in demons. That may be you. If you don't believe what I say, please believe what the Bible says. Jesus casted out demons, so then they are definitely real. Others who may be reading this might think spirits and demons are the same thing. I used to think that way. I couldn't tell the difference. Then I read the Gospels and saw Jesus dealt with demons and spirits differently. When reading Mark 1 and Matthew 8 we see when Jesus dealt with evil spirits, he did not mind if they spoke. However, when it was a demon, he did not let them speak. He clearly had an understanding they were different things. Ephesians 6:12 furthers the discussion between differentiation of spirits and demons.

From my understanding, demons create spirits to weaken us so they can break us down. Isaiah calls spirits "garments" in chapter 61. I believe demons use spirits like clothes in order to get a good hold on believers. I don't believe demons can touch us without a legal right.   Allowing spirits to stay in your life, gives the demon legal rights, choosing to accept the spirit the demon gives rather than believing the fullness of what Jesus did on the cross. My understanding is they send things like a spirit of infirmity to make you sick, or a spirit of confusion, or a spirit of addiction to weaken you. The bible mentions many spirits the enemy uses to break us down: lust, rebellion, religion, slumber, heaviness, haughtiness, fear, bondage, poverty, bondage that leads to fear, etc. If you choose to wear these garments, demons can start to oppress you through these false identities. Matthew 8:16 says Jesus got rid of the demons by casting out their spirits. I believe this is proof that without the spirits on you like garments, the demons cannot stay. This revelation is what I operate in. When I do a demonic deliverance, I cast out the spirits.

MODERN DAY DEMONIAC

Just a week before I wrote this, I performed a deliverance for a young man, who had 8 demons. It took 5 seconds. I was amazed. I did not expect the ease and swiftness at all, but was preparing myself for an all-night battle. I focused on God's love for him, I told him he was loved, and I repeated it. Then, I began to bind the spirits – there were three God revealed to me through a word of knowledge. When I told them to go, the demons left without a fight, it was over. It took me five seconds to name the three spirits and tell them to go. My friend, who had brought him to me, and I spent the next 45 minutes teaching him about the cross and his new identity, removing any potential foothold the devil could use. Then we prayed for him. As my friend was praying, the man's arms lifted. We then turned on some worship music, because he said he hadn't been able to worship God in years. So we cranked up the volume and left the room, with him sitting in a chair, his arms straight up. About 10 minutes later, we went in to check on him and found him still sitting there with his arms still raised. "I can't put my arms down! It's the craziest thing. I can do everything else but that!" All three of us laughed as a spirit of joy had filled the room.

We stayed there for a total of 45 minutes, just worshipping, waiting to see if his arms would come down. Then a song came on that said something along the lines of, "I am loved by God." As soon as that line was sung, his arms slowly dropped. We asked each other why his arms were doing that for so long, but we could not figure it out, so I asked God. Immediately I heard, "How does a child run to his Father?" When I told the guys what I heard, we all teared up. The one in the chair said, "I have been running from God for a while. And I have wanted to run back to God so bad, but didn't know how." We realized his spirit had been crying out and wanting to be held by his Father for so long, that as soon as we started to pray to God, his arms went up. It was a beautiful thing to see and a great lesson for all of us. Love is powerful, and binding spirits is an easy way to get rid of demons. I saw my new friend a few days later, and he was beaming with joy.

LOVE THE PERSON

The most critical aspect of spiritual warfare is loving the person. The next line I am about to write may be challenging. Spiritual warfare is not a fight between you and the demon. That fight was about 2,000 years ago, and it took place on a cross. Colossians 2 says Jesus made a public spectacle of the enemy. Just love the person you are contending for with God's love. My attitude wasn't to get demons out of that man. My goal was to let Holy Spirit invade and move into his heart. If Holy Spirit is there, no demon will come close. That is what happened to me. My ADHD and bi-polar disorder left me the moment my back was healed and woke up from my spiritual coma. I have no room for those past struggles in me. I am filled with the love of God. I try to make sure I am full of Holy Spirit at all times so that God is glorified in all I do.

I have witnessed a few deliverance ministries do their work over the years, and one thing I often find is an attempt to get a demon out. These ministries often have teams of people saying/chanting something along the lines of, "I plead the blood of Jesus," while a leader argues with the demon trying to find out what its name is in order to make it leave. So often, we Christians get tricked into fighting a battle that has already been won. In 2018, I was invited to help with a team of people who had traveled to Nashville, Tennessee to learn how to minister in the power of Holy Spirit. On the last day, while the team was praying for a lady, a demon began to manifest. A few of the team members moved her into a small room nearby and began to try to deliver her from the oppression. An hour later, I was invited into the room. The one in charge was arguing with the demon while the other two were doing the praying/chanting thing. I politely asked the two to step back and to stop what they were doing. Then I asked them if anything had changed in the hour they had been in the room, to which they said no. I then told them they could only pray in silence, but that I would rather they praise God, telling Him how amazing and wonderful He is. I then went to the one who was arguing with the demon and said, "Thank you for what you are trying to do. Do you mind if I give it a shot?" He was relieved, so he stepped back and let me try. I thanked God for His presence in the room, for the cross and what Jesus did there, for authority, and for His love – declaring His love to overwhelm the enemy right there and now. I then called two angels from Heaven to escort the demon back to hell. Immediately the chaos stopped. The woman, who had just been screaming with her tongue sticking out, looked up at me and cried out, "It's gone!" I just smiled at her and replied, "Yeah, honey. Jesus is so beautiful, isn't He?" We walked her to her car, spending a few minutes to remind her of who she is in Christ, and then we got in our van.

"I COMMAND THIS STORM...!"

I was preaching in Kimilili, Kenya in a church with a tin roof and tin walls. A hail storm moved over the church, and started to make a lot of noise as the ice bounced off the tin sheets. It became so loud my interpreter, Pastor Ben, couldn't hear me speaking even when he had his ear up to the speaker. It was at that point I handed him the microphone, and walked outside. I stood out there in the midst of the storm and pointed up at the yellow clouds, "I command this storm to stop right now! I am going to finish this sermon, and you will cease, in Jesus' name!" By the time I returned to grab the microphone from Ben, the hail had stopped, and I finished my sermon. I honestly don't know if I expected it to stop or not. I just knew God was telling me to preach and the racket of the hail storm prevented the people from hearing me. In telling this testimony, I have had multiple people comment about the parallels to Jesus calming the storm. All I know is I believe we have all authority on the earth. I believe Ephesians and Colossians both teach us about the authority we have as believers. Colossians 1 tells us Jesus has all authority and all of His fullness dwells in us and gives us the same authority.

DEFEATING PRINCIPALITIES

I had a dream in June of 2017. In the dream, I stood at the base of a mountain. God told me to climb it, so I did. It took a whole day, but I got up to the top and looked out at the valley below. It was the city of San Francisco. I don't know if there is a mountain near San Francisco, and I don't think that matters. As I stood on top of the mountain, I saw the city, all lit up in the now night sky. Then God told me to look up, so I did. I saw seven dark figures in black, each with a scroll. They were reading in unison. The words I heard were: Cancer, Death, Homosexuality, Poverty, Drug Addiction. As the dark figures spoke a word, it would form into giant block letters, 15 feet tall, and the words would fall on the city. As the letters hit the buildings and streets, they would stick, developing roots to entrench themselves to whatever they were attached to. As these seven beings read their list, I realized they never stopped, never took a breath. As soon as they read through their scroll, they immediately started over. It was a relentless curse.

I was overwhelmed. "God, what can we do against such things?" "Come," He shouted. Immediately, we were somewhere in the city. The big black letters were falling down all around me. Suddenly, God gave me a scroll. I opened it and saw the words: Health, Life, Sonship, Wealth, Freedom. They were the exact opposite of the words falling down. I began to read them out loud. My words formed into white block letters that actually grabbed hold of the black letters and pulled them out of the ground and buildings as they rose up toward the dark beings above me. When the words reached them, they scattered. Instantly, God took me to another mountain and told me to climb. I climbed all day, finally reaching the top at night.

Again I saw a city, this time Tokyo. God told me to look up and I saw seven different dark beings with scrolls. These scrolls were personal to Tokyo, but the words did the same thing as in the previous city, rooting themselves into everything they touched. God took me into the city and handed me a scroll. I read it confidently. My words grabbed theirs and lifted them up to the beings, scattering them in fear. He took me to a third place, Shanghai. I climbed a mountain there, and saw more black beings with scrolls. I was brought into the city and read the one scroll handed to me. And then I woke up. While sitting on the edge of my bed, trying to figure out what it all meant, I heard God tell me, "Every city, town, village, and homestead on the planet has seven beings reading scrolls to curse my people. No one ever fights them. Will you?"

I have since taught about what I learned from this dream at multiple places. One place I taught it was at the village of Soy, Kenya, in August of 2017. It is a small town of about 1,000 people with six Christians who held on to their belief. These faithful few were only allowed to meet in the village's waste hole (our version of a sewer) where they had set up a little tin shed intended to hold corn, their only source of income. The water well in the town was owned and operated by the mosque, and the only way you could get water was to convert to Islam. The only other way to get water was to make a 10-mile trek in the African heat, so most converted. Driving up to the church, the weight of the enemy was so strong I felt it about 3 miles before we even arrived into town. I immediately remembered the dream and asked God "what is causing this darkness?" One at a time the curses over the village came to me and I wrote them down during the car ride. When I arrived at the church, four more non-believers from the village came and so I had a captive audience of ten. So I shared with them my dream, and gave them a list of 12 things I knew were being spoken over the town from what God shared with me. They agreed those were the strongholds over their village and committed to going against it.

A few months later, I was back in Kenya. It was April 2018, and I was there to introduce and teach Vacation Bible School to their church to reach the kids in the village. The two leaders of the church in Soy traveled to see me. They told me they wanted to testify of what has happened, so we sat down under a tree to talk. Because of what I had previously shared with them about the dream and the 12 curses, they decided to commit to every Monday walking down every road in town and speak against one of the items on the list I gave them. I honestly had forgotten what was on the list, so I asked them what they started to speak against. "Witchcraft was first, so we spoke against it every Monday as a group. We would shout 'We declare the death of witchcraft over the city of Soy! Witchcraft is dead, so says the Lord!' every Monday, until our feet had touched every inch of every road in town. At the end of the month, the witch doctor died. This man could not be killed, he would curse people and they would die. He was so powerful, that he used to call everyone in the village together and he would perform powerful signs. He even killed himself three times just to prove that he had power over death. No one dared to oppose him, until you taught us the key. He died within a month. The next day, everyone in town brought us all their witchcraft items and asked us to destroy them. So we burned everything."

"So, the first Monday of October, we attacked item number two, alcoholism. We decided to walk the streets again, ending at the two bars in town. Pastor, the two families that owned the bars were the wealthiest in town. Everyone drank alcohol, even the Imam at the mosque. Well, we started declaring the death of alcoholism. Everyone became terrified of alcohol because our God was serious about it. Within three months, by Christmas, both bars were closed and both families had moved to other towns. We even have a law now that no one can drink. So January we started number three, Islam. We started walking the streets shouting, 'Our God declares the death of Islam!' Soon after, the children refused to go to the mosque. They told their parents, 'The Christian God killed witchcraft. Allah couldn't do that. The Christian God killed alcohol. Even the Imam was a slave to that. We will not worship him anymore. Their God is greater.' So now, we are making plans to build our own church because no one goes to the mosque anymore. When the children stopped going, the parents stopped going. They all come to our little shack."

I was amazed. I was sitting underneath a little tree just outside their church, trying to avoid getting more sunburned, as they told me these testimonies, and all I could reply was, "Are you serious? Did this really happen? Give me more details!" When I taught them about the dream just 8 months prior, I presented with the disclaimer "this is based off a dream and I did not have scripture to go along with it. It's going to sound crazy, but I believe the dream is from God." For it to bear that kind of fruit, I could hardly believe what I was hearing. They were so grateful for what I shared with them that they were trying to honor me, when all I wanted to do was honor them for their boldness, trust and faith in God.

What would the world be like if Christians committed to destroying the principalities that speak curses and enslave us to them? What would your city look like if you began breaking the strongholds? What would your family look like if you spoke life into it, and battled the way God intended you to battle the enemy? I believe it would be like Soy, Kenya. Shortly after these six believers went after the strongholds, God not only added to their numbers, but the mosque and the water well was abandoned by the Muslims and opened to the Christians to now use as their church, holding services and freely giving water away to the people. These few Christians believed what God said, demonstrated His power in prayer and declaration and did not shrink back in the face of persecution or intimidation of others. And in doing so, they watched God deliver their city of strongholds as He brought freedom to the people. We serve a mighty God, friends, and He expects us to really serve Him with diligence, boldness and faith. God is faithful to supply us with the solutions needed to advance His Kingdom, and He chooses us to partner with Him!

Chapter 7

Love

John 4:19 says, *"We love because He first loved us."* I always knew God loved me. I was surrounded by people who taught me how loved I was by God. At a very early age I learned the classic church songs like *Jesus Loves Me*, and *Jesus Loves the Little Children*, I looked forward to attending Sunday School and being at church. I grew up with God. I remember being three years old, and Jesus coming into my room every night and talking with me on the lower bunk bed that I shared with my brother. My brother is four years older than me, so he was already in school, and he would throw pillows from the top bunk and yell at me to be quiet so he could sleep. Jesus' love was always in my life, and I didn't struggled with loving others generally, as it came easy, but I did not love myself. I saw my sin. I saw how detestable I was. I saw how depraved and sick I was. I did not see myself as worthy to be loved, and so receiving love was near impossible. I thought the people who loved me wouldn't if they knew the real me. No one could ever really love me because of a self-perceived darkness that was potentially in me and I needed to cover that up. I knew He loved me, but I couldn't receive it. I loved Him as best I could. And then at 32 years old, I really met God's love.

MY WRONG VIEW OF LOVE

I saw love as correction and discipline. God must discipline me because of my sin. It's why I had a damaged rotator cuff, torn ACL, torn meniscus, broken ankle, even ADHD – I went through all of these aliments because of the sin in my life and that was the punishment. To apply it to others, I believed people who were born blind, had miscarriages, or who lost their jobs, was all due to the sin they were involved in. The law is perfect and if you break the law, you pay for it. I would read scriptures through this lens of judgement to validate my belief. The book of Job and his friends offering "great" advice upheld my case all the more. Spare the rod, spoil the child. That was love. I was all about going out on the street and holding up banners with messages like, "Turn or Burn!", "Repent or Perish!". My classmates growing up heard me say phrases like that often. I was all about telling them if they did not stop their partying and worldly lifestyles, God would smite them. I felt it was my duty to correct them. If you asked me, back then, "But shouldn't we love them?" my answer would have been, "That is loving them. I don't want them to burn. The best form of love is rebuke." That's why the old Jeff, with his way of thinking and view of God, would hate and want to silence this transformed Jeff. Do you want to know what caused my transformation?

It was a simple revelation: I realized even though I did not believe in these things I have written about, even though I had judged and hated people (despite the fact that the Word says not to do either), God loved me so much that He wanted to set me free from me. When God healed me, I realized I was valuable. I actually had this thought, "Wow. God loves me. He actually bankrupted Heaven so that I could fall in love with Him." The transformation was instantaneous; I fell in love with God that very moment. I wasn't serving a vengeful God anymore. I was serving a God of love and grace. Even though I was this disgusting, detestable, lukewarm Christian who thought he knew everything, and felt it was his mission to prove it to the world, God cut right through the religion that promoted my arrogance and touched me. He healed me when I was trying to prove He didn't heal, He moved through me in ways when I didn't think I could be used, He loved me when I didn't understand what love was.

That was so hard for me to swallow the fact I was just learning what love was, because I had preached a series of sermons on the love of God throughout the years in multiple churches as an ordained minister; the difference of man's love compared to God's love, and my entire view was ghastly limited on the love of God, and how we are called to love others. In one second, I realized I had no clue what love was. May I be so bold to say this is probably one of the biggest problems with Christianity, the limited view of God's love. It amazes me that Christianity has a thousand different denominations, and each is convinced it has the best view and defends it, to the point of offending others and scattering the flock.

THE LOVE OF CHRIST COMPELS US

We must always be careful when it comes to our attitude. I cannot emphasize enough how important it is to love. 2 Corinthians 5:14-21 rocked my world. When I saw God's will for me was to see people from a Heavenly point of view, I changed completely. Before that, I constantly struggled with who my enemy was. I would get mad at people, I would lose patience, or yell. I came across this passage the same day God healed me. It was the first scripture God taught me, and it truly set me free from Religion. That passage helped me to see people, not for their circumstance or the sin they must struggle with, but with God's love and compassion.

"For Christ's love compels us, because we are convinced that one died for all, and therefore all died. And he died for all, that those who live no longer live for themselves, but for him who died for them and was raised again. So from now on we regard no one from a worldly point of view. Though we once regarded Christ in this way, we do so no longer. Therefore, if anyone is in Christ, he is a new creation; the old has gone, the new has come! All this is from God, who reconciled us to himself through Christ and gave us the ministry of reconciliation: that God was reconciling the world to himself in Christ, not counting men's sins against them. And he has committed to us the message of reconciliation. We are therefore Christ's ambassadors, as though God were making his appeal through us. We implore you on Christ's behalf: Be reconciled to God. God made him who had no sin to be sin for us, so that in him we become the righteousness of God." 2 Corinthians 5:14-21

How beautiful! The love of Christ compels you and me to love like Him. Jesus died for everyone, for all. The last I checked, the word "all" really means all. It doesn't mean all believers, it means all people. He died for all so that all might stop living for themselves, and would start living for Christ. Do we? Are we really living for Jesus? Are we living a life that looks like the life He lived? If Jesus switched with you right now, would He handle things differently than you? You see, I know how difficult it is to consistently live up to that standard. It doesn't change the fact that we must! I want to live for Jesus, I want to be His ambassador, I want to introduce people to Jesus. Verse 16 taught me how: to no longer see people from a worldly point of view. This implies that from now on I will see everyone from a heavenly point of view.

A MINISTRY OF RECONCILIATION

When God looks at a sinner, what does He see? Does He see wrath and judgement, or does He see what He made them to be? Does God see their potential? Maybe that's why He heals a kid with a broken wrist despite knowing what censored words will come out of the boy's mouth. Maybe God loves people so much that He looks past the mistakes they make. Maybe that much love is a good thing? God gave us all a ministry and that ministry isn't a pulpit or a church position. The ministry we have all been given is a ministry of reconciliation. 2 Corinthians 5:18-19 says we have all been given a single message to proclaim: God no longer counts men's sins against them. Are we reconciling a lost world to its loving Father? Are we showing God's love in a way that truly represents the Cross? Or are we trying to focus on us, instead of the Cross?

God's love was greater than I had believed. Remember, I come from a place where I believed God's love was punishment, forcing me to not do fleshly things, pronouncing warnings to people; I thought that's what God wanted from me. When He healed my back and legs, I was overwhelmed with the fact He had actually healed me, mainly because all the things I thought God used to discipline me, He removed; the injuries I thought God gave me to keep me on the straight and narrow, He healed. What I thought was always from God, was never from God. When I started praying for people and showing them the love of God I had come in contact with, and telling them He is not affected by your sin, He is not concerned with your sin, He is concerned with you knowing Him. I personally don't care if you continue sinning, but let me pray for you, and your natural response will be to stop sinning because you will realize He is a lot better than you thought He was. I am not going to concern myself with your sin, but let me paint a different picture of God than what you think He is, let me show you how kind He is, let me show you how good He is. And the results were staggering. I watched atheists give their lives to Christ, Hindus and Muslims, back-slid Christians, bawling their eyes out because of God doing things they never dreamed of. And it was based off of the passage of scripture in 2 Corinthians 5. The more I did this the more I began to realize, not just in theory, but in application, that God is even greater than what I then thought. I would come across young people that were doing things opposed in the bible, but while they were doing it, I would introduce them to the love of God, all the while they were angrily complaining of who they believed He was. I would introduce them to Father God, they would typically respond with a burst of bad behavior, God would move, they would then apologize and give their life to Christ. Right In the middle of the sin was God's love to erase all of it. It's amazing how much better Holy Spirit is about bringing repentance than we are.

THE TRUTH THAT LEADS TO REPENTANCE

Friends, if you learn anything from my book, I want you to learn one thing. God's goodness will lead men to repentance. We must stop teaching John the Baptist's message, and start teaching Jesus' message. John was the one who yelled, *"Repent! For the Kingdom of God is near!"* Jesus taught, *"The Kingdom of God is here. Heal the sick, raise the dead, cleanse the lepers, and cast out demons. Freely you have been given, freely give it away* (Matthew 10:7-8). *Forgive, love your neighbor, love your enemy, and pray for them."* Jesus flipped the message. I know that Matthew 4:18 says Jesus preached *"Repent for the Kingdom of heaven is near."* What I am trying to say is once His ministry progressed, He didn't teach His disciples to preach "Repent". He taught them to prove the Kingdom is already at hand. He even pointed out in Matthew 12:28 the things he was doing proved "the Kingdom of God has come upon you." Because of this, I believe Jesus' message progressed from "Repent, for the Kingdom is near," to "Look and see, the Kingdom is here." The Pharisees killed Him for His message.

The Western Church is set up in John's ministry, not Jesus' ministry. At some point, we must break free from tradition and look like Jesus. Our church must look like Jesus. If your church doesn't always look like Jesus, don't leave the church, love the people. Become the embodiment of Jesus and show them a better way with your love. Don't talk about it, don't argue with them about it, don't attempt to persuade them. Prove God is better than they know through demonstrations of love through Holy Spirit, like Paul did in Corinth. Live the Gospel. Love people so passionately that whatever they are struggling with gets removed. God is a loving Father, and He desperately wants His children to know His love. See people from God's eyes. See their created value. Don't see them in their lowest point, carry hope for them. Show them how much God loves them. Set the captives free. I love that as soon as Jesus left the wilderness, he went to the synagogue and read Isaiah 61. You and I have been given the same task, as if God was making His appeal through you.

"The spirit of the LORD is upon me, because the LORD has appointed me to preach the good news to the poor. He has sent me to bind up the brokenhearted, to proclaim freedom for the captives and release from darkness for the prisoners, to proclaim the year of the LORD's favor and the day of vengeance of our God, to comfort all who mourn, and to provide for those who

grieve in Zion—to bestow on them a crown of beauty instead of ashes, the oil of gladness instead of mourning, and a garment of praise instead of a spirit of despair. They will be called oaks of righteousness, a planting of the LORD, for the display of His splendor." Isaiah 61: 1-3

This is our calling. This is our ministry. We get to set people free, the same as Jesus did. We get to see people healed.

It's amazing to watch a person get out of a wheelchair, to see a tumor shrink before your eyes, to see someone lose 45 pounds while you pray, to watch bones grow. I love it. It's even more amazing to see someone fall on their knees and tell God they are sorry. It's amazing to see someone get set free from an addiction to drugs or pornography. It's amazing to see a city stop practicing witchcraft, and be set free from the snare of alcoholism.

LOVE REACHES THROUGH ALL CULTURES AND RELIGIONS

It is also beyond my wildest dreams to witness Muslims and Hindus accept Christ. I have seen quite a few of these over the past few years. One young man came to our Indian Fellowship a few years ago, as a Hindu. He didn't understand it was a Christian group, he just heard Indians come to worship God in Telegu, which is his language. I preached about Jesus that night, and afterwards he approached me saying, "I understand Jesus is real. I see Him on you. But my gods are real, too. They have answered my prayers before." We talked for a little while about Jesus, and then he left, promising to come back. A month later, our church hosted a conference. On Saturday night, while in worship, I heard God tell me to run to the back of the church. I didn't want to because I was enjoying the worship. I heard the command again, so I turned to run to the back. I got about halfway there when this same Hindu jumped into the aisle and proclaimed,

"I must talk to you now!" I took him out the doors to the front steps. Once outside, he told me, "How do I choose? If I choose Jesus, who I know is really God, I will lose everything: my family, financial support and I will never be able to go home. If I don't choose Jesus, I will have all of that, but not Jesus."

I joyfully replied, "It's not a choice. The Lord, through you, will lead your family to Him if you let Him." I shared Acts 16:31 *"Believe in the Lord Jesus and you will be saved, you and your household."* As I'm sharing all of this, out of the corner of my eye I see my friend John Park getting off a phone call, so I motioned for him to come over to us. I asked the Hindu to share his dilemma with John, and as he did, John looked at me with a big smile and gave his response,

"It's not a choice. The Lord will save your family through you if you let Him."

This Hindu was stunned when he heard us answer the same way. We both continued to pour into him the Love of God. It was there on the front steps of the church that he gave his life to Jesus, no turning back.

"HAVE HER CALL HIM RIGHT NOW"

There was a day in 2016 where I decided to go back out on the street with water bottles to pray for people. It had been a few months since I had been in front of the church praying. I was out there alone that day, and the amount of traffic was a lot less than in 2015. I prayed for about 50 people that day, and one was an atheist. At first, he came up to me to argue. I don't argue. I listen to what they have to say, and then commend them on their argument. After I do that, I share my testimony, and many other stories such as these I have mentioned here in this book. After I did, I asked him what he thought. He didn't know what to think, and just stood there in silence. I then asked him if he had anything I could pray for so God could prove Himself to him. He stated he had not talked to his mom in years, and if God would make his mom call him right now and apologize for everything she did to him, he would be open to believing God existed. So I prayed, "Father, I thank you that you love this man. God move in his mother right now and show her she needs to apologize to her son. Have her call him right now, so that he knows that you love him and want a relationship with him, amen."

As soon as I said amen, his phone rang. I smiled in awe as he pulled his phone out of his pocket with wide eyes and looked at his screen that said "MOM" was calling. He looked at me with bewilderment as his phone continued to ring, and I had to tell him "answer it!" He answered, in disbelief, and all I heard on the other end was, "I am so sorry..." He freaked out, tears came into his eyes, and he told his mom, "I got to call you back", and he hung up on her. Those tears were now pouring down his face as he hung up and collapsed into me, fell on his knees, and said "God *is* real." He gave his life to Jesus right then and there. He then called his mom back and apologized for hanging up, and while he was apologizing she interrupted to tell him,

"it's ok I need to tell you something, I met God a few weeks ago, and accepted Jesus last week."

He responded, "I just did that, that's why I hung up on you." They cried together with an understanding God had healed both their hearts and their relationship was restored.

Another atheist gave his life to Jesus that same day. He was in a hurry, so I was actually running down the street with him on his way to class. I asked him if I could pray for anything, but he said he was fine. So I asked him if I could bless him and thank God that he had no need for prayer. He agreed as we jogged. I prayed for him, and had a word of knowledge about a few things. He stopped as my prayer ended, and said, "I have never met a Christian who believed like you. You are absolutely convinced that God is real." We began walking again, and I asked if what I said in my prayer was accurate, and he verified that it was. I asked him what he thought about the fact that I knew those things, and he stopped again,

"Yeah, that is pretty crazy. I'm not sure what to think."

"The God you don't believe in told me. I have a relationship with Him, and He speaks to me. He knows everything there is to know about you, because He loves you. He wants a relationship with you, too. Would you like to meet Him?"

"Yes I would love to meet God, if he exists."

"He does. Here, let me pray so that He will make Himself known to you. I am going to ask God to give you a peace you have never experienced before."

I prayed and God did give him peace. The young man gave his life to Jesus right there on the steps of the college engineering building. Love people. Get Heaven into them. The enemy lost a long time ago. No fight is necessary. We just need to go after Jesus and His love.

LET HIM HEAL YOU

We love because He first loved us. If anyone says he loves God, but hates his brother, then the love of the Father is not in him... This was me. I thought I loved God. I thought I knew what love was. Friends, let this be a checklist for you, if nothing else. If you are judging someone, not forgiving someone, or holding resentment toward someone, then the love of the Father is not in you. Let that junk go, and embrace the love of the Father.

Let His love change you. Realize Love keeps no record of wrongs, and forgive people for whatever they have done. If Jesus was able to say on the cross, *as they mocked Him*, "Father, forgive them, they know not what they do," then so should we. "Forgive, but never forget" is not the Gospel guys. Sounds like wisdom, and I thought it was before I encountered love. Forgiveness is not forgiveness unless it completely lets go and allows itself to be vulnerable again. The reason we do not "forget" is because we do not want to be hurt again. But, we cannot forget Jesus actually came to set us free from hurt. Hurt is a spirit that isn't from God. God heals the broken, and He binds up their wounds. If you are trying to protect yourself from hurt, then you are being your own god in that area of your life. He is our comforter. Let Him heal you. Go to Him with your pain and struggles and say whatever you need to say to Him, but in the end, let Him have control. Why? Because He loves you! And you cannot receive His love if you don't love everyone. If you don't love everyone you see, then the love of the Father isn't in you. Read it for yourself in 1 John 4:17-21, it is wonderful.

THE ONE THING THAT COULD SEPARATE US FROM THE LOVE OF GOD

In order for us to love everyone, we must be filled with His love and gain an understanding of how far His love goes. It knows no ends. Paul revealed something very powerful when He was writing his letter to the Church of Rome. In Chapter 8:37-39, Paul starts this section with the "we are more than conquerors" quote. Often times, that is all I hear people quote from this passage, but we must not forget the rest of the sentence! *"...through Him who loved us."* It is all about LOVE. Then he writes an awesome list of the things that cannot separate us from His love: death, life, angels, demons, present, future, powers, height, depth, not anything in all of creation. When I read this passage, I see something missing from this list: *past.* My past can keep me from the love of God. It used to. I hid from my past, and tried to hide my past from everyone else. My past kept me from feeling worthy of love. I am tremendously grateful God showed me something that helped me get free of my past. God doesn't keep a record of my wrongs because He died for my sins. He set me free from the one thing that kept me in bondage, my sin. I realize now, God bought my past BECAUSE it was the one thing that could prevent me from encountering His love. He bought my past, and He wiped me clean of it.

The gratitude I have because of His love inspires and compels me to love Him in return. And just as important, it inspires and compels me to love everyone I meet, regardless of what they look or smell like, what they believe, or how they treat me. Jesus said the Truth would set me free, and it really has. I am finally free from my past, and the Jeff that hated himself. I now realize that Jesus' love for me set me free from me, and because of that realization, I can actually deny myself and follow Him. Love has become a habit for me. Love is what drives me because I've learned His love is transformational.

Chapter 8

Signs and Wonders

G od loves to bless His people. We have seen a lot of incredible, supernatural things at the church in the last four years that there's no clear reason why, but I can only assume happened because God wanted us to know He is there. For example, on July 1, 2017, I got a text message from our custodian at the time that simply said, "What do I do with this?" accompanied by a single picture. The picture was of his finger, and a small diamond on the end of it. My first reaction was to ask if it was real. He was not sure what it was. Then I asked him where he found it. He found it on the floor next to a pew. I asked him if it was the only one, to which he wasn't sure. A few moments later I received another text from him that said there was a diamond beside every pew! He said they were each placed in the exact location in relation to every pew. I told him to put them in a bowl near the altar at the front of the stage. The next morning, which happened to be Sunday, I got to the church and ran straight inside the sanctuary to see them. The diamonds were still there, and 14 more were found on the floor that morning. We put them all in the bowl, and I told everyone we would leave them there for as long as they remained. I never encountered this before, and didn't know of anyone else who had, so I was totally clueless, but something inside of me told me they were not permanent. I wanted to see how long they would last. If they manifested out of thin air would they disappear the same way? After church service, I stayed in the sanctuary to worship. I was the only one in there for the entire afternoon. At 5:00 p.m., I looked in the bowl to find it completely empty.

"WHO THREW A PARTY HERE LAST NIGHT?"

The next Saturday, our custodian sent me a text that asked, "Who threw a party here last night?" When I asked him what he was talking about, he sent me a picture of the back two pews. They were covered in a green glittery dust. He said, "I have been vacuuming it for hours, but there is so much I can't clean it all." I told him to stop what he was doing and to leave it there. The next morning, I again ran inside the sanctuary with excitement to look at it. Most of the green glitter was gone, but it looked like tiny pieces of emerald, ground up into a type of green sand. It was beautiful. Everyone marveled during church. It stayed for a few days before it all disappeared. About a month later, gold glitter showed up all over the floor and pews. The gold stuff, which we now call gold dust, still manifests on the 7th pew to this day.

In December 2018, our church was hosting a small group meeting with 20 people in attendance. I was in the back running the A/V system while one of our students taught. The student invited me up to give some commentary so I walked up to the front, spoke for about 5 minutes and walked back to the sound system, and as I did I saw silver glitter on the ground, and my thought was "someone must have spilled something", but I continued to walk. As I took a step, a thought came into my mind "No, I am manifesting" so I turned around and went back to look, and the small pile of silver glitter was now 3 times its original size and watched in awe as it looked like it was continuing to grow and spread.

Then I heard the Lord say, "hold out your hand and catch it", so I held out my hand and looked up at the ceiling and waited for glitter to burst through our ceiling tiles, with child-like faith wondering where it was going to fall. I was running back and forth with my eyes fixed above and ready to catch it. I heard the Lord say, "this is faith", I never saw the dust fall from the ceiling, and I eventually got confused about it and stopped, and asked God "when are you going to do it?" To which He replied "I already have." That phrase did not make any sense to me, so I looked down at my hand and there was a single gold speck in my right palm below my ring finger.

When I saw that one little speck, it shot forth faith and I yelled out to the group shouting, "God is manifesting now! Get back here now!" When I looked down, there was gold dust everywhere, on the back pews and carpet. We all marveled as it still continued to grow. It began to change color, the silver turned to gold and gold to silver; and one person in the group said "I don't believe this is real" and so she said, "if this is God, I want Him to make the dust green" and in that instant, like a wave, it all turned green. By this time six pews were covered in the colored dust and it was still growing. Then it changed to purple and when it changed purple, another girl exclaimed, "No way! I just told God in my mind if this was real, turn the green to purple!" Then the dust finally turned to blue, and that's when we saw an outline between the blue dust in the pews of angel silhouettes!

In all of our glee, one of our girls said "do you think we can see diamonds? I been praying for God to show me a diamond", and I said, "sure, I don't see why not, let's start looking for diamonds." About five seconds later she found one. Then everyone started searching and by the end of the night we had a total of 40 diamonds appear: 33 were white, and 7 were pink. We also found a single emerald shard. So instead of putting these diamonds in a bowl, we placed them in an alabaster jar with a lid on it and thought, "Let's see how long these last." We were never possessive of the diamonds and invited anyone to look and touch them, and over the years with kids and curiosity, we're still left with a few. It's a humbling reminder that God gives us the desires of our hearts, and when He manifests His presence, it can be accompanied with heavenly treasures. We're not trying to go after the manifestations of diamond, we're just after Him. Again, I can't explain it, all I know is sometimes, a sign will make you wonder.

HORN OF OIL

We have had a few things show up during our praise time, too. One day, after the message, we had a time of ministry where I invite people up to be touched by Holy Spirit for healing or whatever they needed. There were about 30 people who came up, so I started praying for them with the help of a few others. I worked down the line, and came up to a young woman. I started to pray for her, and as I did, a clear liquid like oil started to manifest on her hands. The oil dripped off her hands to the floor. This was the first time I had ever witnessed this manifestation before. We were both surprised, but also confident God was indeed working on her behalf. It always fascinates me because it comes from nowhere. Oil doesn't always just appear on hands. We've had it manifest on windowsills in our sanctuary when a prayer team came on a Friday night in August

2021. My intern called me to tell me as they prayed, oil manifested, and when Sunday came it was still there! The oil stayed for a couple of weeks after that.

In September 2018, we had a 24 hour worship service. I took my shofar which I bought in Israel, planning to blow it every hour as part of an offering of worship to King Jesus. I was with my wife and a friend in the back of the church, wanting to practice first and get the sound right before I did it in front of everyone. As I took a breath and brought the ram horn up to my mouth to blow, oil immediately covered my face. It took me a second to figure out what was happening and why my shofar was not cleaned out. My wife said, "It looks like oil!" She reached out and touched my face to confirm that's what it was and with delight told me she had just read a few minutes ago Psalm 104:15 *"God makes[...]oil to make his face shine."* For 12 hours, every time I picked up the shofar, oil would pour out of it. Every hour I had to drain the oil into a cup so I could blow it for the worship service.

I have seen what we call glory clouds manifest in a church service. Seemingly, out of nowhere, a cloud of gold dust just appears and begins to move around the room. If I could describe it I would say it's almost like a cloud of gnats. I have witnessed it once, when I was at a conference in San Antonio at the Presence Conference, Misty Edwards was speaking, and while she was reading scripture, suddenly over her right shoulder, I saw a gold cloud start to move almost like it was alive and dancing. I couldn't believe my eyes at first, so I asked the people besides me and they saw it too. Misty continued to preach and the cloud just intensified becoming bigger in size. I haven't found a scripture that would give clarity or understanding to the glory clouds, but I don't think that we should discredit it. Ezekiel saw the glory of God leave the temple in Ezekiel 10 and return in chapter 40. He didn't describe what it looked like. In Exodus, God's glory led the people in a cloud by day and a pillar of fire by night, meaning His glory changed its appearance depending on the time of day. Who's to say God's glory only has two modes of manifestation? For me, these rare glory clouds are just another confirmation of God's presence amongst a people.

GOD DELIGHTS IN HIS CHILDREN

While we are producing signs and wonders, introducing a lost world to its loving Father, God is producing signs and wonders as well. I have found God uses signs and wonders to show His pleasure for His children. When a church is pursuing God in a correct and new way, He blesses them with confirmations. I have seen videos of people getting new teeth, of manna showing up spontaneously, and of pillars of light appearing in a church. I can't explain it. I simply believe God is pleased when His children pursue Him passionately. I believe He does crazy, illogical things when people walk in faith and not by sight. I think God delights in His children and loves to bless us with confirmations.

DOUBT IS OK...FOR A SEASON

I don't understand most of these things. Signs and wonders... like I said before, sometimes a sign will make you wonder. I understand people are skeptical. Doubt is ok. Even after Jesus rose from the dead and spent 40 days with the disciples, some of them doubted. It's the verse before the Great Commission, there in Matthew 28:17, *"When they [the eleven disciples] saw him [Jesus], they worshipped him; but some doubted."* I've reflected on this passage quite a bit; here is Jesus, resurrected, doing all these miracles, the net full of fish on the side of the boat for the second time already, walking through walls, appearing and vanishing out of thin air. He has done all these things, and after all of that, Jesus comes to them in Galilee and the 11 disciples are worshiping him, yet at the same time some of the eleven are doubting him and Jesus doesn't correct their doubt. Jesus knows they are doubting, but He doesn't even mention it. Instead, Jesus says to them, "*All authority in heaven and in earth has been given to me, therefore, go and make disciples of all nations...*" Doubt is ok for a season. What is important is we don't stay in doubt. It was in their doubt that Jesus sent His followers into the entire world to make disciples of the nations. He did not condemn their doubt. The reason is because doubt has nothing to do with faith. Doubt and faith are not in opposition to one another. The opposite of faith is sight. I have doubted many things, whether they are true or not. That is why it's good to investigate something when you have doubts. Test things out. Don't hide in fear about it. Wrestle with that thing until you know if it's fake or real. If you doubt glory clouds, gold dust, oil manifesting, and diamonds are from God, then go seek it out for yourself. Go to where you hear about it, and find out for yourself rather than just dismissing the idea because it's uncomfortable or sounds impossible.

God knows your intentions. If something is good, it will produce good fruit. If it is bad, it will produce bad fruit. Good trees cannot bear bad fruit, and bad trees cannot bear good fruit. Find out what kind of fruit something has and you will know whether it is good for you or not. Don't take my words for it, test it for yourself. Get some experiential knowledge, like 2 Peter 1:5 says, "*For this very reason, make every effort to add to your faith goodness, and to goodness, knowledge.*" Doubt all you want, but don't stay in your doubt. Find out the truth. That's what I did. I was full of skepticism and doubt about healing. I thought Todd White was a heathen. I was certain he and people like Benny Hinn would be in hell someday. I thought my now good friend Robby Dawkins was an insane idiot who worshipped a contorted, twisted version of God that would someday result in absolute judgment. In my doubt, I decided I needed proof. And God proved I was completely wrong. And that caused me to ask, "What else don't I know?" I have been on a quest to remove all the doubt in my life. If someone mentions instruments playing on their own in a room during worship, I want to see it and find out for myself. I want answers, not assumptions.

SIGNS THAT SHOULD FOLLOW US

What is more important than the incredible signs I have mentioned, are the signs Jesus told us to be ready for. In Mark 16:15-18 Jesus gave some final instructions. In those instructions, Jesus mentioned some signs of believers:

"And these signs will follow those who believe: In my name they will drive out demons; they will speak in new tongues; they will pick up snakes with their hands' and when they drink deadly poison, it will not hurt them at all they will place their hands on sick people, and they will get well."

Those are some pretty impressive signs. They are supposed to follow all who believe. We need to drive out demons. That is completely possible. It's scary, but as we've learned Love conquers fear. We have the authority over the enemy. Jesus made sure we were aware the enemy was under our feet. Another sign is we should speak in new tongues even though a lot of people think tongues ceased. I used to be a cessationist and thought all the gifts stopped. My experience told me God didn't do miracles. My theology professors told me they had stopped. The only time I had witnessed miracles was in other countries. I justified it because I was in places where the gospel had not been established, and once the people believed in Jesus, the miracles would cease just like back home in America. At least that's what I always assumed.

LET GO OF FEAR

Now, I know what a fool I was back then. I have experienced a lot of miracles. Nothing has ceased. A lack of miracles is just evidence of someone operating in fear of the unknown, just like I used to. It is time for us to let go of fear and pursue love. The whole snake thing is crazy, isn't it? And the poison thing is like, "ok Jesus, you lost me." I am reminded when back in July 2018, I took a team of people, including my friend John Park, to Yucatan, Mexico to teach the Gospel to the Mayan people. On the last day, I sent John and 7 others to the village of X-Katun. While they were there working VBS, the townspeople started to bring food and drinks in celebration and thanks-giving to our team, for all we had done during the week. When they brought some homemade punch, John was worried about it because we cannot drink their water. No one had really gotten sick the whole week, and we definitely didn't want to risk it now. John suggested that no one drink the juice. That's when one of the ladies of the village came over and told them, "A gift from Jesus will never make you sick." They all drank the punch, and no one got sick from it. John told me about it later that night. It isn't the same thing as drinking poison, but the water will really make you sick down there. The last sign that follows those who believe is the laying on of hands to heal the sick. This sign is incredibly powerful for those to encounter God. None of the signs Jesus is looking for are small, insignificant, or comfortable. Our choice is either to ignore Jesus' counsel by dismissing their importance, or we learn to do what he says. In order to do that, fear has to go. I could not justify ignoring this scripture any longer, and neither can you.

FOLLOWERS OF THE WAY

Basically, Jesus, in Mark 16, is explaining what He's looking for in His followers. The original believers weren't called Christians, the Greeks gave them that name. The Jews named believers Followers of the Way. I love that. They didn't just believe in Jesus, they followed His teachings. They didn't just talk in theory, they demonstrated Jesus' way of life. They performed miracles. Peter, John, Stephen, Philip, Paul all did amazing things because they were followers of the way of life that Jesus taught. They understood Jesus was expecting them to perform signs and wonders. John 14:10-14 teaches us more:

"Don't you believe that I am in the Father, and that the Father is in me? The words I say to you are not just my own. Rather, it is the Father, living in me, who is doing his work. Believe me when I say that I am in the Father and the Father is in me; or at least believe on the evidence of the miracles themselves. I tell you the truth, anyone who has faith in me will do what I have been doing. He will do even greater things than these, because I am going to the Father. And I will do whatever you ask in my name, so that the Son may bring glory to the Father. You may ask me for anything in my name, and I will do it."

We can learn a lot from this passage. Even when it came to Jesus, He wasn't the one healing, but it was the Father in Him that healed. It is the same with us. The Father, living in me has healed countless people. It is the Father's work to heal, cleanse, cast out, and raise. He does it through us, just like God did through Jesus. Jesus' prayer was that we would be in God the way He was in the Father, and the Father was in Him. I want that. I want to remain in Him, and I want His words to remain in me. I want to do what Jesus did. I want to see you do what Jesus did. Jesus told us we will do greater things than He did because He would be with the Father, contending for us (John 14:12-14). We can command storms to dissolve. We can pray for rain to stop for three years, like Elijah did, and then pray for rain again. These are the signs God is looking for in us.

"JESUS CHANGED ME"

A pastor friend of mine named Chris Donald, visited our church for a conference and brought about 10 of his students down to help with outreach, as well as to gain some experience in ministry. After the Saturday night session, Chris and I were really hungry. So I took him to Whataburger (if you haven't eaten at one, just know it's a little piece of heaven on earth). Chris is always ready to share the Gospel with someone, and as we went inside to order, he shared with the cashier. We ordered, and then went to sit down. "Liz" brought the food to us. She asked us if there was anything else we needed, and Chris went for it. He began to tell her the gospel. She called herself a "pagan." She confessed she had never read the Bible, but she talked as if she had. She lashed out at the "inconsistencies in the Bible" telling us that we were fools for believing it.

That's when Chris really stepped up. He told her he wanted to introduce Jesus to her. If she would let him pray, Holy Spirit would actually rest on her and she would know Jesus is really God. He asked for her hand, which she gave him confidently assuring herself nothing would happen. He prayed a simple prayer like, "Father, you love Liz. Touch her so she knows you really do love her. Amen." As soon as he finished praying, he told her he had a vision of her battling anxiety and suicide. She immediately tried to pull her hand away, and looked at both exits as if trying to escape. I could see the fear in her eyes, and knew she thought we were psychic or something, so I stepped in to assure her that it was Holy Spirit that showed him the vision he saw.

Chris then went on to tell her more, after he assured her, "I am not going anywhere for at least an hour. If you decide you would like to talk some more, I will be here. If not, don't worry about it. Just know Jesus loves you, and He is pursuing you." Liz went back to work, and about ten minutes later, Chris' crew came in. They apparently noticed Holy Spirit on Lisa, and asked her what was going on. She told them she felt hands on her shoulders ever since Chris had prayed (she told us that she felt nothing). One of the guys from Chris' team came over to us and pointed to her and asked if we had prayed for her. When Chris said yes, he responded with, "Chris, she just gave her life to Jesus!" Lisa came to our church the very next day, and didn't miss a single service until she got a new job in Austin. The very first Sunday she came to church, my wife and I gave her a ride home. Kate walked her to the door, and when her mom opened the door, she commented, "My goodness, Lisa, you look like a different person!" Lisa responded, "I am mom. Jesus changed me. I am a new creation." My wife reported how Lisa's mother could tangibly see her daughter's joy and complete change of character. No more depression, no more anxiety, no more suicidal thoughts, no more "paganism", all of it changed in an instant from a sign from Holy Spirit.

Chapter 9

Pharisees

The reason I started off the book calling myself a Pharisee is because of the attitude I had before I woke up from my spiritual coma. The Pharisees were totally against the miracles Jesus taught. They hated the miracles, because it proved His way was right. Jesus' message was not like the message of the Pharisees. Jesus taught to turn the other cheek. Jesus taught to love everyone. Jesus taught status and prestige was worthless in the Kingdom of Heaven. Jesus constantly used the Pharisees as examples of people who missed the point. The Pharisees tried to trap Jesus constantly, asking him about taxes, washing hands, etc. In Mark 12:13, there is a passage where the Pharisees ask Jesus a question. His reply is, "Why are you trying to trap me?" If you want to see how Jesus felt toward the Pharisees, read Matthew 23.

THE RIGHT THINKING

When I woke up from my spiritual coma, I realized I was a Pharisee: I lived by the law. I spent my whole day focused on me and the 10 commandments. If I didn't break them, I had a good day. If I broke one of them, it was a bad day which ended with me begging God for forgiveness. I judged everyone, including myself. I made fun of anyone who didn't believe what I believed. I tried to convince everyone to believe like me. I loved to argue. When I went to other churches, I spent the whole time scheming for a way to prove them wrong. Look, I know there are wrong teachings in every church, and I try my best to correct ours at my church.

I now look past differences in beliefs, and I just focus on showing Jesus to everyone I meet, including other pastors. If they ask me questions about my beliefs or interpretations, then I answer them honestly. But I don't yell at people, I don't try to argue with them, and I don't try to talk myself approved. I don't want to be a Pharisee any more. I don't want to spend my entire life listening to a sermon, wishing I could make someone else listen to the message because they need to hear it. So many people have that attitude, it is quite a disease. We have to break free from this way of thinking. It is not how God thinks. God wants us to think about Him, and to work on our relationship with Him. He does not want me to be thinking, "Man, I wish Jimmy was here right now to hear this message because it would help him so much." Instead, God wants me to think, "I am so glad I am here this morning, because I needed to hear this sermon. And even more importantly, I need to put it into practice immediately."

Jesus was radical. I mean, Jesus was doing some really crazy things compared to the Jewish establishment. He was constantly crushing everything they were doing. He healed people. They had a problem with that. Pharisees had a problem with healing. I used to have a problem with healing. Then, to top it off, He healed on the Sabbath! They really had a problem with that. He then forgave the man's sins! They had a problem with that. His followers didn't wash their hands. The Pharisees confronted Jesus about that. He didn't follow their law the way they taught it, and yet He still didn't sin. They really disliked Him for that. He knew the scriptures better than they did. No matter how hard they tried, He always confounded them. They schemed to kill Him, and then they had Him killed.

I know I was a Pharisee. I wish I could somehow help people see they are Pharisees. Unfortunately, I find many of the Christians I meet are Pharisees. They follow the law more than they follow Jesus. They aren't followers of His way of life. They have their checklists that make them feel good about themselves. They go to your church, and spend more time judging others around them than they do worshipping God. They concern themselves with stopping people from bringing food or drinks in the sanctuary, how much dust is in the windowsills, and how much food someone brought (or didn't bring) to the monthly potluck lunch, instead of worshipping God, loving everyone that entered the room, thanking God that someone gave of their time to clean what they could, and the fact that hungry people were fed a meal.

CONSUMED WITH THE WRONG THINGS

That was me. I was consumed with appearance. I was consumed with the law. I was consumed by sin. I evaluated myself all the time, to see where I was sinning. I was consumed with justifying myself, proving I was holy, and judging others as less holy. Today I am not sin-conscious. That means I do not think about sin. Whether I sin or not, I do not think about it afterward. Like Paul wrote, I forget my past and strive towards the goal. I live every second in effort to look like Jesus, to love like Jesus, and to live like Jesus. I want people to see Jesus when they see me. I want Christ in me to reconcile people to their loving Father. I have found when I focus on God's love, I don't sin much. I focus on Righteousness, not Holiness. Both are incredibly important, but Righteousness bears unto Holiness (Romans 6:22) which means Righteousness produces Holiness. Holiness doesn't produce Righteousness. Righteousness is the tree, Holiness is fruit the tree bears. I don't try to be Holy. I did that for 25 years as a Christian. I failed every day. Now, I try to be Righteous. Jesus was Righteous. He is the Righteous standard set before us. That's what we all need to be. We need to live righteously, and that will produce the holiness we all seek. Righteous living is living a life of love – in love with our Father, loving your neighbor as yourself.

What about the Law, you may ask. Jesus, Himself, said that He didn't come to abolish the law but to fulfill it. The law isn't dead! Please read Galatians 3. It changed my life. Verse 25 states, *"Now that faith has come, we are no longer under the supervision of the law."* The whole chapter is amazing, by the way. Paul really wrote a powerful message, under the influence of Holy Spirit. He wrote a similar message in Romans 6, with the big sentence being verse 14: *"For Sin shall not be your master, because you are not under the law, but under grace."* I believe these verses prove my point. I was a Pharisee because I was consumed more with the law than I was with the Spirit. I thought I was supposed to teach the law and live by it, and I thought everyone who talked about Grace and the Spirit was a lunatic. The Law was my god, without ever realizing it. Now I know Jesus was a radical, and He wants me to be radical. Jesus wants Radical to be normal; he wants us to look nothing like the world. He wants me to live a crazy life that is so different from an unbeliever it prompts them to ask questions. I don't want to blend in. I don't want you to blend in. I want you to look different. He wants you to look different. He doesn't need Pharisees, He needs Peter walking to the temple with his shadow healing people, walking right past the same Pharisees who hung Jesus on the cross.

"DIABLO! DIABLO! NO!"

Every summer, our church goes to a part of Mexico to work with the Mayan people. It was a work my grandfather led for 25 years. When he passed away, I stepped in. The churches down there are very traditional Southern Baptist. They have discouraged miracles, signs, and wonders. They have only preached from the Old Testament, because they are consumed with the wrath of God for the unholy and wicked. On one of our more recent trips, we had a little problem occur. On the last night of the mission trip, one of our groups stayed back at our home base church as they were finished working for the evening. Marlyna, one of the young women in our team, saw across the street from the church a party was going on. She didn't know who lived in the house, but God gave her a word of knowledge for a girl inside. So Marlyna and an interpreter walked across the street, went inside the house and found out it was a birthday party for the same girl she had the word of knowledge for. The birthday girl was turning 18 and everyone was drinking alcohol to celebrate her being legal to do whatever she wants. Suddenly, Marlyna heard shouts from outside, "Diablo! Diablo! No!" The voices outside were shouting for Marlyna and the interpreter from our team to get out of the house. When she came outside, they told her the people were not holy people, and if she stayed inside it would ruin the reputation of the church. It caused a great conversation between the members of our team and the members of the church.

We cannot be so consumed with being holy, with our reputation, that we miss our purpose. God created us to be His hands, feet, and voice. Yes, He wants us to be holy. But we can't miss the point of life. We are supposed to reconcile a lost world to a loving Father with a single message: "God no longer counts men's sins against them." If I am consumed with holiness, I will never understand this point. What was Jesus' focus? Was Jesus consumed with not sinning so that His testimony wouldn't be invalid, or was Jesus consumed with showing people the Love of the Father? Then why should we be any different? Since that night, we have seen an amazing transformation in the church, and the same lady who called the neighbors the devil, goes over to the house to build a relationship with those people in order to show them how amazing God is.

LOIPOI

Pharisees got it twisted. Pharisees still get it twisted. Pharisees think God is consumed with wrath and anger for sin. I did a word study of Ephesians 2:3 one day. It says because of our sin, we are objects of God's wrath. I looked up the Greek word for wrath, because I felt God tell me it was important. The Greek word written there is "loipoi," which means an extreme sadness or depression, as in the loss of a loved one. That is a far cry from the angry wrath of God we have all been taught about. Paul, who was a Pharisee among Pharisees and believed in a vengeful and angry God, wrote God is saddened and heartbroken by our sin. Just a few verses later, it says we are saved by grace. Saul was a Pharisee, he wanted to hunt down Christians and kill them. Paul was not a Pharisee, he was a Follower of the Way. When he encountered the loving Father of Heaven, He was changed forever. There was no going back. It's the same for me. Since I woke up, I've noticed a transformation in how I read scriptures. I can read a scripture I've read my entire life, but now I'm able to see it in a new way. I don't see God's warnings or anger like I used to, but rather I see the joy of God, the excitement of His heart, the beauty of His love.

THE PETER BEFORE AND AFTER

Before I woke up, I related more with Peter before Pentecost than after. The old Peter always put his foot in his mouth. He was so much like me. Most people I know relate to that Peter. I always heard people say things like, "Peter makes me feel like I'm ok." Then I read about him in Acts. Man, that Peter was totally different than the one in the gospels. And if you really want to see change, read Peter's writings. Wow! Talk about radical! The Peter of the gospels denied Jesus because he was afraid. Jesus was taken to the Sanhedrin, put on trial, and there was Peter in the back of the room – the exact same location where he denied Jesus three times. Just a few months later, Peter was captured and put on trial by the Sanhedrin, and while on trial, proclaimed to all of Israel Jesus was the Messiah, the miracles he had done were in the name of Jesus, that the Sanhedrin had killed the Messiah, and they were the evil men God had prophesied about, telling it all to their face, knowing that doing so would probably get him killed. When we line up those two passages of scripture we see how much Peter changed. And what was the cause of his transformation? He was filled with the Holy Spirit. He stopped being consumed with behavior modification, and he began to put the love of God on display. I want to relate to that Peter, the one who was transformed from a bumbling fool to a bold lion. I want to be the one people line up for with hopes that his shadow would heal them. I want to be Paul, not Saul. I don't want to be a slave to sin. I want to be a bondservant of righteousness. I want to keep the Faith. I don't want to be a Pharisee. I know I was a Pharisee. I would have hung Jesus, right beside Todd White, Robby Dawkins, Will Hinn, and many others...right beside the Jeff I am now.

Chapter 10

Opposition

S o much of Jesus' time on earth was spent preparing His disciples for persecution and rough times. The reason Jesus said "The Son of man has no place to lay his head," was to prepare people for the cost, and hint at the lonely life they would have. There's two ways to look at walking with Jesus: to look sinless, or the other side is being compassionate and loving while partnering with Holy Spirit. The more we try to look like Him, or the more we try to live out the book of Acts the more persecution will come. There's a reason why the people who get the closest to the throne of God are the ones who have been persecuted and martyred for their ability to look like Jesus (Revelation 6:9-11). I have encountered a tremendous amount of opposition in the last few years, and there are times I feel like I have no one else near me who understands (I know this isn't true, but it feels like that sometimes). I have mentioned it throughout this book, such as with my father on Father's Day. What I haven't mentioned is is I have had church members slap my bible out of my hands after demanding I prove with scripture what I believe and teach is found inside. I have been punched on the street by someone for trying to pray for them. I have actually been pushed to the ground by another former member of the church because I wouldn't respond with anger toward him as he tried to entice me to lose my temper. These oppositions all came about over the gifts of the Spirit in 1 Corinthians 12:7-11. It's interesting to me how I can preach the law all day long and no one gets upset, but if I try to teach people how to partner with God in order to set themselves and others free, people want to attack me, threaten me, and convince others to leave the church. It doesn't matter how much they've grown in the Lord or how much they've seen others transform in our church. For many people, once they cross that line because of something I've said in a sermon, nothing I do seems to help. I have had many pastors, from multiple churches, tell me I have lost my mind. I personally take that as a compliment because I have found in the bible where it says not to think like a man, but to think like God (see Matthew 16:23). I want to use the mind of Christ, not Jeff's mind. If I have lost my mind, it is proof that I am in His. It can't get any better than that. Some of the Christian ministry leaders on the college campus across the street from our church have told their students for years to stay away from us because we are false teachers. We still provide them lunch and financial support.

In April 2019, there was a campus wide worship service, in which I was asked by one ministry to help lead. In an attempt to build relationships, I gave my suggestions to the host ministry, that they should invite all the other ministry organizations on campus and delegate to each group small tasks to help, instead of us since it was a campus service. The two largest organizations both stepped up and helped tremendously, which is great. We came to support the event, and I brought about 20 people. Before the event, I was talking to a student who attends one of the campus ministries and volunteers there. We talked for over an hour about the bible, as he was all about proving his worth through works and quoting great theologians of the past. I asked him what book of the Bible he had been spending the most time in lately, but he couldn't answer. He told me about the other writers he had been reading, how they said this or they said that. I asked him again which book of the Bible he had been soaking in. He asked me what I meant by soaking. In an attempt to clarify, I asked him a few questions. Which book had God been opening up to him while he was in prayer? Which book was it that he felt compelled to read constantly? Which book was giving him deep revelations about Jesus? Again, he had no answer. So he asked me which one was I in, and I spent about 15 minutes talking about my latest revelations. He stated that he could tell I love the Bible. I took that as an open door and shared for another 20 minutes about all that the Word does for me, and how I think the Bible is the most important book he can ever read. It was a great conversation. He asked so many questions. Our time was running out, as it was almost time to get started, and I needed to meet with some other people there, so I excused myself and talked with the guy in charge of everything.

When I had finished speaking with him, there was an announcement for us to go to the left side of the room, so I began walking. I passed the other young man I had spent so much time with, and he was talking to his ministry's leader. As I did so, I couldn't help but hear their short conversation, "What did Jeff say to you?" "Oh, he would only talk about the Bible, and the many miracles, signs and wonders he has seen." "I told you, he is false. Stay away from him." I was actually right beside the leader as he said this, so I reached my arm out and placed my hand on his shoulder, and said, "I love you man. God bless you, brother." He turned white, and I kept walking.

Our church, just a few years ago, had 40 college students. Now we struggle to have 10. This is because of the college ministries. They consider me to be false. They openly tell their students to stay away. Sometimes, students from our church go to their worship services or small groups, and come back with questions like, "What did you do to the campus ministry leader? He hates you. He spent time telling me how bad you are, and how you are leading me astray." This happens every semester. That same night, a woman came up to me to rebuke me. When she got in my face, I affectionately smiled at her and held out my hand, because I had never met her before. She froze. All she could say was, "Thank you." That was it. She walked away with bewilderment.

I have been spoken about, screamed at, spit on, slapped, and threatened. I will never hold those things against anyone. It's important for us to remember Jesus told His Father to forgive those who mocked him while he died on the cross. It is also important for us to remember Jesus said you are blessed if you are persecuted because of Him. Look, I am not trying to be a martyr here. I am not trying to make anyone feel bad. I am simply trying to show you the cost of living out the gospel, free from religion. I have had pastors call me, from my own denomination in town, and tell me I have to stop praying for people and close our Healing Rooms. When I tell them of the miracles, the success rate, and all God does for the people, they always reply with, "Wow, I had no idea. That is amazing. Keep it up." As Jesus said in John 14:11, *"Believe me when I say that I am in the Father and the Father is in me; or at least believe on the evidence of the works themselves."*

I had a pastoral meeting at a restaurant with a guy who got kicked out of a Baptist Church for similar stories to mine. During the meeting, a man walked into the restaurant and recognized my friend, and was unaware he had been removed from the Baptist church. He asked my friend if he was in town to preach at his church, and my friend replied, "No, but I'm back in town, I'm just serving at another church." Then he tried to introduce me to this guy, and when the man heard the name of the church that I pastor, he looked confused, turned to my friend, and asked him, "Why are you associating with him? (gesturing to me), Don't you know who he is and what he does?" Then he turned to me before my friend could answer and said, "Why do you still have the name Baptist on your church, when no one at your church is Baptist and you're completely false?" My friend stepped in and said, "Actually, I got kicked out of the Baptist church and that's why I serve at the Pentecostal church now, and Jeff follows the bible more closely than anyone I have ever met at your church, have you ever been?" The guy didn't know what to say, and walked away. It feels like a constant wave of ridicule, from people who have no idea who I am or actually what goes on in our church.

FAMILY FEUD

My family has been the hardest, though. I have had my parents, my aunts, and cousins call me to tell me to stop. They talk about me behind my back. My parents, at first, were very critical. But now, they know it is good. My dad actually made a statement a few years ago that truly stuck with me, "I have always secretly struggled with Christianity because it just didn't add up. But Jeff, since you got healed, I have seen more and more make sense. Now I see it all, clearly, and finally I have something worth giving my life to." With my close friends and family there comes these moments of breakthrough and revelation and it's beautiful and encouraging, but that spirit of religion is relentless, and many times tradition is comfortable and it's easy to revert back to.

My family is similar. When I am with them, they act as though nothing is wrong. But they talk about me all the time. They call my brother, my parents, or me to show their concern. I typically get yelled at, but my parents and brother just get concerned conversations. I feel bad for them, but my parents also, now, believe in healing. They pray for as many as they can. My brother is not completely on board, which really makes me feel bad that he has to deal with other family members. Persecution is real. I've been yelled at by people with picket signs and megaphones. I've been called a false prophet. I've been told I will experience the wrath of God like Annanias and Sapphira, by strangers. Before I woke up, I would have joined them. I can't say it enough, if Jeff from before April 2015 met the Jeff of today, he would hate me with a vengeance. He would no doubt get physical with me to threaten me and stop me from continuing in my pursuit.

My grandmother was amazing. She supported me more than I could have hoped. I'm sure it wasn't easy for her to come to terms with some of the things I do now, but she knows my heart. She has always been a rock for me. The rest of my family is hit and miss. To my face, they are great. But then I hear of things they supposedly say to others. Either way, I don't care what they say, I love them. I know they don't all agree nor do I need them to. Some of them think I have lost my mind or gotten persuaded by the Pentecostals. I understand, I was just like them for 25 years. Sometimes, they seem genuinely interested in gifts of the Spirit, only to lash out and spend hours trying to put me in my place. It's like they never actually listen to what I say. For example, on multiple occasions I've had family text me a question about some biblical topic and we will text for 12 hours, all positive and they ask questions and it seems like we are getting somewhere and agreeing...only to later have a seemingly planned moment where they snap, mock me, say I'm false, tell me I'm going to hell. I won't lie, these conversations cause tremendous pain. It takes a while, with many long conversations with the Lord to get refocused. I will always be hopeful though, and the door for conversation is open no matter the agenda on their end.

I've told you all the good, sweet things the Lord has done, but there is a cost. Andy Stanley said, "Believing in Christ will cost you nothing, but following Christ will cost you everything." I learned it's at these times one of the costs of following Christ is your family and friends and even other churches won't understand. I've learned the enemy uses those closest to me to make me try to question my calling and walk my faith out.

Opposition is real, be prepared. Persecution is guaranteed when there is relationship with God. What I want to do here is encourage you not to settle for the approval of man. Follow Jesus. Let that be your purpose. Let that be your whole mission in life. Strive to be an Imitator of God. I know I say it often but reconcile a lost world to their loving Father. Let God make His appeal through you. Love people who persecute you. Bless people who oppose you. Walk with the character of God. Be His imitator and representative on earth. Don't give in to what the enemy says. Don't believe lies. People, no matter how evil they seem, are not your enemy. People are loved by God. He wants them to know His love. Let Him use you.

Chapter 11

Unity

This may be the single-most important topic and it's rarely written about. What does it really mean, and why is it so important? Jesus prayed in John 17:21 and verse 23 for us to be one, in complete unity. I have to admit, knowing Jesus prayed for you and me 2,000 years ago is a pretty powerful thing. Realizing His prayer was for us to be one, as They are one, is life changing. Jesus' desire and heart cry was for oneness. "May they be in complete unity..." Guys, unity is important to Jesus. At some point, we have to come together and stop the divisions. It seems that today's Christianity is so divided. We have our own churches, and it has gotten so bad that if someone disagrees with me, they leave and start their own church. Did you know there are over 4,000 different Christian denominations on the planet right now? I remember reading that in an article back in 2017 there were only 1,000 denominations then. When are we going to realize religion is all about isolation and separation? How is it possible for 1,000 denominations to become 4,000 in a five-year period? The enemy is simply trying to divide and isolate us so that we can't be united.

Why does it always have to be a "you versus me" thing in Christianity? Why do we draw these lines of "your belief is wrong, so you must be a false teacher"? Why is this our go-to behavior, why such anger and over-the-top division? Why can't we simply just be willing to test things for ourselves? Why can't we have some civil conversations, acknowledge our differences, continue to love despite them? We hardly ever look at people's fruit; we either agree with a teaching and think the world of someone, or we disagree and do all we can do in our influence to discredit them? Where is our love, and where has unity gone? Why does it feel like many Christians try so hard to go against Jesus' prayer in John 17?

It is a terrible reality to see Christians hating each other, to the point of resentment. I used to be like that. When I saw Benny Hinn, I would think about how crazy he seemed. I still haven't met Benny (and don't have plans to do so), but I have met his nephew and his son-in-law. His nephew, Will, is someone I now call a friend. He has come to our church and led a conference. I met him at a conference because of Robby, and I had no clue who he was. He seemed like a normal, good guy. Then, about 6 months later, I was in my office and stumbled on an interview with him, and God told me I would meet him in three days with the purpose of inviting him to the church. I thought to myself, "No way! He's a Hinn. I can't bring a Hinn to a Baptist church!" But God told me, "In three days, you will invite him." So I figured that if I somehow ran into Will Hinn somewhere in three days, I might as well invite him. Sure enough, on day three, there he was, standing beside me at a conference in Austin! I was stunned to say the least, but I knew what God had said to me so I invited him, and he was excited about the chance to come! His ministry is actually dedicated to bringing churches of different denominations together to worship in unity. He says, "Jesus is perfect theology. We may differ on a lot of things, but Jesus is what unifies us."

God's Kingdom is all about family, love, and unity. Satan is all about stealing, killing, and destroying, isolating people with fear, worry, anxiety, and jealousy. Think about it, what did the first sin cause Adam and Eve to do? They hid from God. Their sin caused isolation. When you and I sin, if we do not have a proper foundation of the Gospel, we will feel guilt, shame, or even condemnation. That is because guilt is designed to make people expect judgement. So, in order to avoid people judging me, I feel compelled to run away, or hide. That is human nature. When we sin, we hide from God. When we sin, we hide from our brothers and sisters. That isn't the Gospel. The Gospel says that *there is no condemnation for those who live in Christ Jesus* (Romans 8:1). It means that nothing separates me from the love of God. There is no reason to hide. There is no reason to run away.

Where sin abounds, grace abounds more (Romans 6:20). That isn't a license to sin and get away with it. It's an invitation to *taste and see that God is good* (Psalm 34:8), because *His goodness leads us into repentance* (Romans 2:4). The more I see how good God is, the more I will want to honor Him with my life. The more I encounter His grace, the less I will want to abuse it. The more I realize God just wants a relationship with me no matter what bad things I do because of His great love for me, the more I will love Him in return. It's amazing what God wants to do in our lives. And we need to be united in order for that to happen.

So often, I see young people, just like I used to be, make a mistake and respond by disappearing for a few weeks or months. Eventually, I find them living in another city, living completely in sin, giving up on God. In order to help them find freedom, I go to where they are and hold their hand. I remind them of God's great love for them. Jesus leaves the 99 to after the one. So must I, in order for them to see His love. It's amazing how quickly you will see people come back to the Father, in true repentance and love when you love them back. It's so much better than a bull horn and a picket sign. I've never heard anyone come to God that way. I have never heard someone say, "I want what you are presenting to me" to someone with a picket sign.

My closest pastor friend is from an Assembly of God church. I am from a Baptist church. I know pastors who are free like I am free from many different denominational backgrounds. It is such a beautiful thing to see churches come together to worship. Every Easter, in our town, the Assembly of God church puts on an amazing Passion Play. For the last five years, our church has been honored and blessed to have a part in it. Do they need us? No. They have done this play for about 25 years. But it is just a blessing to see churches come together to present the Gospel. There is a beauty in the unity.

We, as Christians and representatives of Heaven, have got to stop the judgement of other churches. We have got to come together and serve the community. I promise you this: If a city's pastors would come together and go out in public and actually practice the Gospel, praying for healing, giving prophetic words, etc. it would change the culture of the whole place. Think of the impact! Churches, going out into the community, not to just invite them inside the building, but actually going out and loving on people would be the greatest sight. And if multiple churches, and even better, multiple denominations, got together to serve people and love them it would destroy ridiculous hostilities. Not to mention, we don't even understand what other denominations believe. I can't tell you whether Catholics actually worship Mary. I know I have been told they do. I know it appears they do. But there is a difference between honoring Mary and worshipping her. I can't tell you what the Catholic doctrine about Mary is. I don't know what the Episcopal Church teaches and believes. I've learned what the Methodist Church believes because I preached in one for over a year. I have learned a lot about the Assembly of God church beliefs because of my good friend, Pastor Ed. At the end of the day, our doctrines (the things that separate us) won't lead us into deep intimacy with God, only what unites us can do that.

We need to quit criticizing denominations because we are different, and instead focus on our similarities. My church hosts a conference roughly every six months. When we do, I always invite every church in town, as well as many others in the surrounding area. I have invited up to 80 churches for a pastor's meeting to talk about unity in the body. Of those 80, only 3 showed up, counting myself. It was heartbreaking, hence why I am adamant to talk about unity. I don't host conferences so I can convince people what I believe. I am trying to bring churches, the Body, together. I am trying to unite us. God has placed a burden in my heart to unite the Body. I am not trying to convince people to join our church. I want people to see we are not bad. I want other churches to see we are a church that supports and loves them. We see value in every church. We must be unified. Scripture says one day, the Church will be.

The way I see it, the Church is the Body, and Jesus is the head. It's scripture. I believe the Body has to be in direct proportion to the head. I don't think God wants a disproportionate body. He did not intend for the Church to be a tiny, broken, stick-figure that argues amongst itself about which is the best. He intended for us to be unified, strong, together, centered around Jesus, loving the lost. He wants us to be warriors for Him, and an army of Love. One day, we will wake up and unite.

Chapter 12

The Secret Place

Psalm 91:1 says, *"He who dwells in the secret place of the Most High God shall abide in the shadow of His mighty wings."* I love the secret place. I have amazing encounters with God there. I want you to know my secret place isn't my closet, my office, or my bedroom. It is where I dwell. The passage says, "He who dwells..." What does it mean to dwell? It means to set up permanent residency. We are supposed to dwell in the secret place. The problem I found was I only visited it occasionally before I awoke. Even after I woke up, I wasn't dwelling in the secret place for over two years. I didn't know about it. I had my quiet time, and still do, but I didn't know about the secret place. I spent hours upon hours reading scripture, but that isn't my secret place. In the psalm it says whoever dwells there shall *abide* in the shadow of His wings. The word abide stood out to me when God showed me this verse. I recognized it from Jesus' teaching: *"If you abide in me, and I abide in you..."* I like that word, abide. It's the verb form of the word abode, which means a place to live. So, whoever sets up a permanent life in the secret place of God will live under His shadow. I was intrigued the first time I read this.

I asked myself, "How can I put this into practice?" My bible says Psalm 91 was written by a priest in the Temple. So someone who lived in the Temple of God wrote this Psalm because of the insight he had gained from living there. He wrote it as someone with experience. The Temple was special because God lived there. Today there is no Temple of the LORD, but we are His temple. We are where He resides. He lives in us and through us. In Ezekiel 36:26 God says, "*I will remove from you a heart of stone and I will give you a heart of flesh.*" I believe this refers to the secret place, shifting from a physical location to our hearts. That is why your quiet place is not your secret place. The secret place is in the shadow of His wings, which implies it can only happen in His presence. Quiet time, is where I get my soul quiet, it's where I quiet my thoughts about anything else and place them on God. I have a quiet place too, but this is not where I receive the revelations my spirit desires. Your secret place is where your heart is, it's where you intimately worship the Lord. If you look at the scriptures that describe Heaven's throne room, you see a place of worship. The psalms are songs to God. I believe if I was to enter the throne room of God, I would not only find worship, but the result of worship, which is peace. I believe the Secret Place is a beautiful place. Remember, heaven is a spiritual place, which allows it to be accessible even now on earth, which is why and how the book of Hebrews tells us we can boldly enter into the Throne room of God.

When I learned about the secret place, I became a radical worshipper. I mentioned before I isolated music in my past. I got rid of anything that was emotional, because of fear that I may lose control. Now, I love to worship. One of my favorite things to do, when I am at church is to play drums or the piano.

I honestly can't tell you if I am good or terrible at either instrument, but I love to play to the Lord. I have played drums most of my life, as I was a percussionist in school. But the piano is something very different. I always wanted to play the piano, so my parents hired a piano teacher to give me three lessons when I was 10 years old. 20 years passed and I never learned any more than those three lessons, but the desire never wavered. In 2014, I began praying for God to connect me to someone who would teach me to play, but no one ever came. In 2019, I prayed that prayer one day and heard a response, "I have given you the ability. Go play." I went to the sanctuary of our church and placed my hands on the keyboard, "Put your thumb here. This is middle C." Over the next three days, I had lessons while I was praying. God taught me music theory, hand placements, and chords. Since Christmas of 2019, I have played piano for the majority of our Sunday services. I am not technically beautiful or classically trained. But I love to play. As for my voice, I was kicked out of the choir when I was 17 because I can't sing very well. For a while I never sang out loud, but now I sing all the time. If I feel nervous about singing, and feel a fear that someone will hear me, I turn toward the person and sing louder. If you ever see me turn toward you and sing, it's because I am worshipping to conquer fear. I definitely don't do it to bless you with my remarkable voice. I know my limits, and I know my God loves when I sing to Him. I am a radical singer. Worship isn't just about music. Worship is prayer, and prayer is worship. I spend my whole day in conversation with God. God never stops talking to us. Not ever. We simply have to train ourselves to know His voice and follow it. Jesus said the same thing, "*My sheep listen to my voice; I know them, and they follow me,*" in John 10:27. I have learned to live in the secret place, in the presence of God. That doesn't mean I always do. There are times where I get selfish and do what I want. I still sin. I make a lot of mistakes. As soon as I do, I am reminded by Holy Spirit, I confess it, apologize, and go back to worshipping Him.

Worship is so much more than singing and praying. I worship God as I mow my grass, and while I wash the dishes. Worship is a relationship, a lifestyle. When I am in my secret place I breathe in grace and I exhale love. I give grace to those who need it, I bring peace to the storms. When I walk into a house, I want the presence of God to fill the place. I want to be used by God. I want people on airplanes to know my God simply because I brought Him on the plane. I want God to be glorified, always, in every situation.

In May 2019, I was invited to Atlanta to do some training for a church group. One morning, I got up around sunrise, and the person I was staying with had a small brook in his backyard. I grabbed my bible and walked down to the crystal clear water in order to spend time with God reading scriptures, meditating on Him. Now, before you chalk this up as a relaxing getaway and an easy quiet time to be with the Lord, let me just say, my host I was staying with lived directly across the street from a drug dealer and crack house. The entire time I was out by the brook reading the word, I was also clearly hearing in the background two prostitutes fighting about, let's just say stuff, which prompted the drug dealer to come outside with a pistol and tell these two women to put on clothes, that they had to leave because people were trying to sleep, all the while these two women were yelling back to collect their money. What a scene. It was far from a quiet and relaxing place in the physical, but I was sitting there with the Lord and as far as I was concerned we both had our feet in the brook and we were having a wonderful conversation in the secret place. I stayed there as long as I could, and then went back in the house to get ready for the last day of training. As we arrived at the church and walked up the stairs to the room where we were supposed to meet, we heard singing. There was a group inside practicing for church the following day. They were good, and so we asked them if we could join them in worship. Suddenly, one of the young ladies saw me from across the room and she stopped everything to come give me a hug. She said, "Oh my! You are in love with Jesus! I can see it all over you. You spent time with Him recently. Wow!" I just smiled and said, "Yes ma'am, I have...and I can tell you have too." In which she confirmed she had. You can tell when someone has spent time in the secret place because of the gentleness, kindness, peace, and joy they carry with them. It's as if Love flows from within them.

My secret place is my absolute favorite place to be. I love walking toward a closed door and saying, "God, I know you are on the other side, and I cannot wait to join you in there!" One Sunday, I was preaching on how God loves to manifest His presence for us, and I felt nudged to demonstrate this in the natural. We have a side door on the stage, so I pointed to it and allowed my spirit to get really intimate with God. I said, "I know you are on the other side of this door," really quietly. Then I turned to the people and said, "I believe God is on the other side of this door." And then I walked toward the door. I opened it up about three inches, and said, "Hey God." The presence that came out from the other side was immense. Just about every person in the first four rows of the pews felt it like a wave. Many people were slain in the spirit right there on the spot. One person there had never encountered anything like that before, and they were quite skeptical. When the presence of God hit them, they began to cry. These same people told me after the service that it was the most powerful thing they had ever encountered and that they were going to make a room at home into a secret place so they could do that every day.

In my secret place, I learned about prayer. God led me to

read passages where Jesus and the disciples/apostles prayed. They always prayed with such authority. They never prayed, "Oh God, if it is Your will, will You please..." Their prayers were always, "Lazarus, come forth," or "In the name of Jesus, rise up and walk." It didn't matter whether it was a prayer for healing, deliverance, or anything else, they prayed with a command. I don't know why people pray, "If it is Your will, please..." Romans 12:2b says,

"Then you will be able to test and approve what God's will is—His good, pleasing, and perfect will"

I should know His will. I should have His mind. I should think, act, and desire what God desires. I should walk in the spirit. I should keep in step with the spirit. The only way that I can do this is to diligently and purposely seek these things, daily, in my secret place. This is where transformation happens. This is where my mind and heart get set on things above. I do not receive transformation from books. Books are meant to encourage you and open your mind up to new things. I am transformed and my mind is renewed in the secret place. It was in my secret place that I fell in love with God. Every good thing I have been given from God in the last seven years (personal healings, baptism of tongues, deliverance, the prophetic, revelations) has been found when no one else is around, with the presence of God surrounding me, while I tell Him how much I adore Him. The number one request I have for God, while I am in my secret place, is, "Father, I love You. Enhance my gratitude. Show me more so that I can be more grateful to You." The deep revelations of the Lord keeps me hungry and excited, so the second thing I always ask God is for new revelation or deeper understanding, however that looks. The reason I say, "...however that looks," is because I cannot know what new revelation or deeper understanding awaits you or me. It's like looking into a dark void, filled with the unknown. We can stand at the edge and look in, but we don't know what's on the other side. We have to take a leap of faith, and we have to do it with God. It can be terrifying, to say the least. I've shared most of my new revelations and deeper understandings with you in this book. When I go to God in prayer and ask Him for more, new, or deeper...I don't know what it means or what it entails. I just know there is more available, more just beyond my sight. Basically, I'm asking God to take me by the hand into a place I've never been before. Like Ezekiel 47, I'm asking God to take my hand and lead me into deeper waters. There is an infinity of things for us to learn and explore with God. It's all available to you.

Chapter 13

Closing

M y hope is that somehow this book helps you to know it is okay to seek God in new ways. My hope is that somehow, you grow closer to God. If you are afraid of one of the things in this book, I hope you at least have the ability to find out for yourself. Don't go to your pastor for advice. Go to God! Seek Him. Find out for yourself. My prayer for you is that you become a blank canvas, forgetting everything you have ever been taught. Go to God, like I did, and say, "Father, I don't know what to believe. So many men say different things about You, and I just don't know what to think. Father, make me a blank canvas. Write Your truth on my heart. Erase everything that is not of You that is in my heart so that Your truth is all there is. Father, I want You to be my teacher." Start at His feet, on your knees, with tears falling from your eyes, as mine are falling now. Let our Father love you into truth. If you need to, wake up from this coma you are in. Get out from the bondage of sin and death, from the law that we were never meant to follow. Follow Jesus. Seek His beautiful face. Oh, that you may know Him more today than you did yesterday! Oh, that you would become a radical, passionate follower of the Way. Oh, that others would see His light in you, and would be moved to more. Your Father is proud of you. Be encouraged! Be strong! I love each of you, and I bless you in Jesus' name.

Oh, my God. I love you with all I have within me, Father. Thank you for calling me to write this book. Thank you, Lord, for helping write it, and for the directions because I could not have done it without You. Use it for Your Kingdom. I pray You are glorified. Father, touch hearts with this book.

About the Author

Jeff Hilliard has served the Lord for the past 12 years in full time, originally traveling as a missionary to several nations. He and his wife, Kate, are have been senior pastors of Kingdom Church in Kingsville, Texas since 2014, and have a ministry focusing on equipping and training individuals, as well as churches, in healing, power evangelism, and prophetic ministry.